TURNER
ON TOUR

Christine Riding

With contributions by
Thomas Ardill | Aimee Ng

National Gallery Global, London
Distributed by Yale University Press

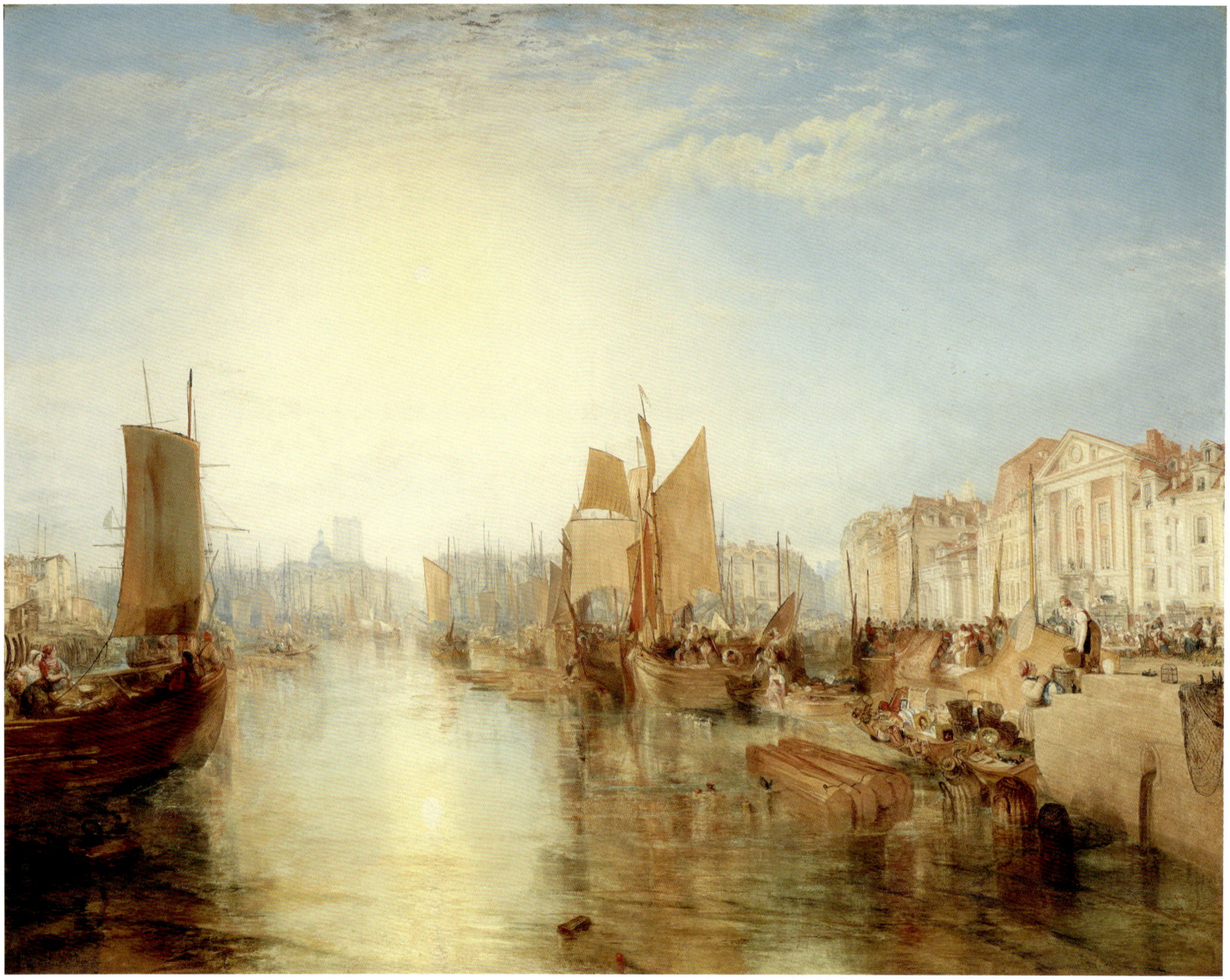

Joseph Mallord William Turner (1775–1851),
Harbour of Dieppe: Changement de Domicile,
exhibited 1825, but subsequently dated 1826,
oil on canvas, 173.7 × 225.4 cm, The Frick Collection,
New York. Henry Clay Frick Bequest 1914.1.122

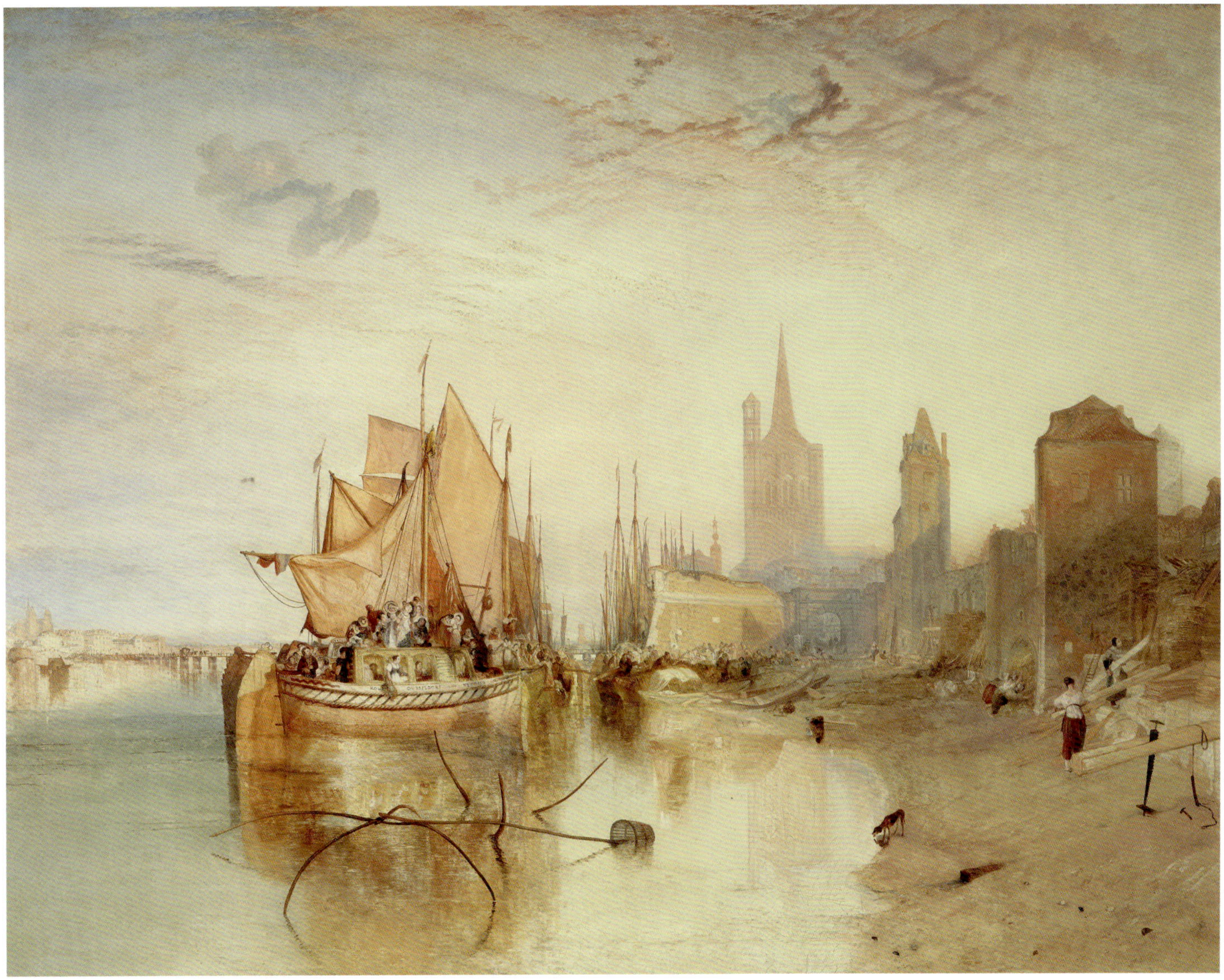

Joseph Mallord William Turner (1775–1851),
Cologne, the Arrival of a Packet-Boat: Evening, 1826,
oil on canvas, 168.6 × 224.2 cm, The Frick Collection,
New York. Henry Clay Frick Bequest 1914.1.119

Published to accompany the exhibition:

Turner on Tour
The National Gallery, London
3 November 2022–19 February 2023

The H J Hyams Exhibition Programme
Supported by The Capricorn Foundation

This exhibition has been made possible by the provision of insurance through the Government Indemnity Scheme. The National Gallery would like to thank HM Government for providing Government Indemnity and the Department for Digital, Culture, Media and Sport and Arts Council England for arranging the indemnity.

First published in 2022 by
National Gallery Global Limited
Trafalgar Square
London WC2N 5DN
www.shop.nationalgallery.org.uk

ISBN: 978 1 85709 689 7
Product code: 1051427

British Library Cataloguing-in-Publication Data
A catalogue record is available from the British Library
Library of Congress Control Number: 2022939972

Publisher: Laura Lappin
Project Editor: Catherine Hooper
Editor: Camilla Rockwood
Proofreaders: Robert Davies and Bridget Harley
Picture Researcher: Suzanne Bosman
Production: Jane Hyne and Justine Montizon

Designed by Adrian Hunt
Origination by ALTA, London
Printed in Belgium by Graphius

All works are by Joseph Mallord William Turner unless otherwise stated.
All measurements give height before width.

Front cover: *Cologne, the Arrival of a Packet-Boat: Evening* (detail from cat. 2)

Back cover: *Harbour of Dieppe: Changement de Domicile* (detail from cat. 1)

THE NATIONAL GALLERY

THE FRICK COLLECTION

CONTENTS

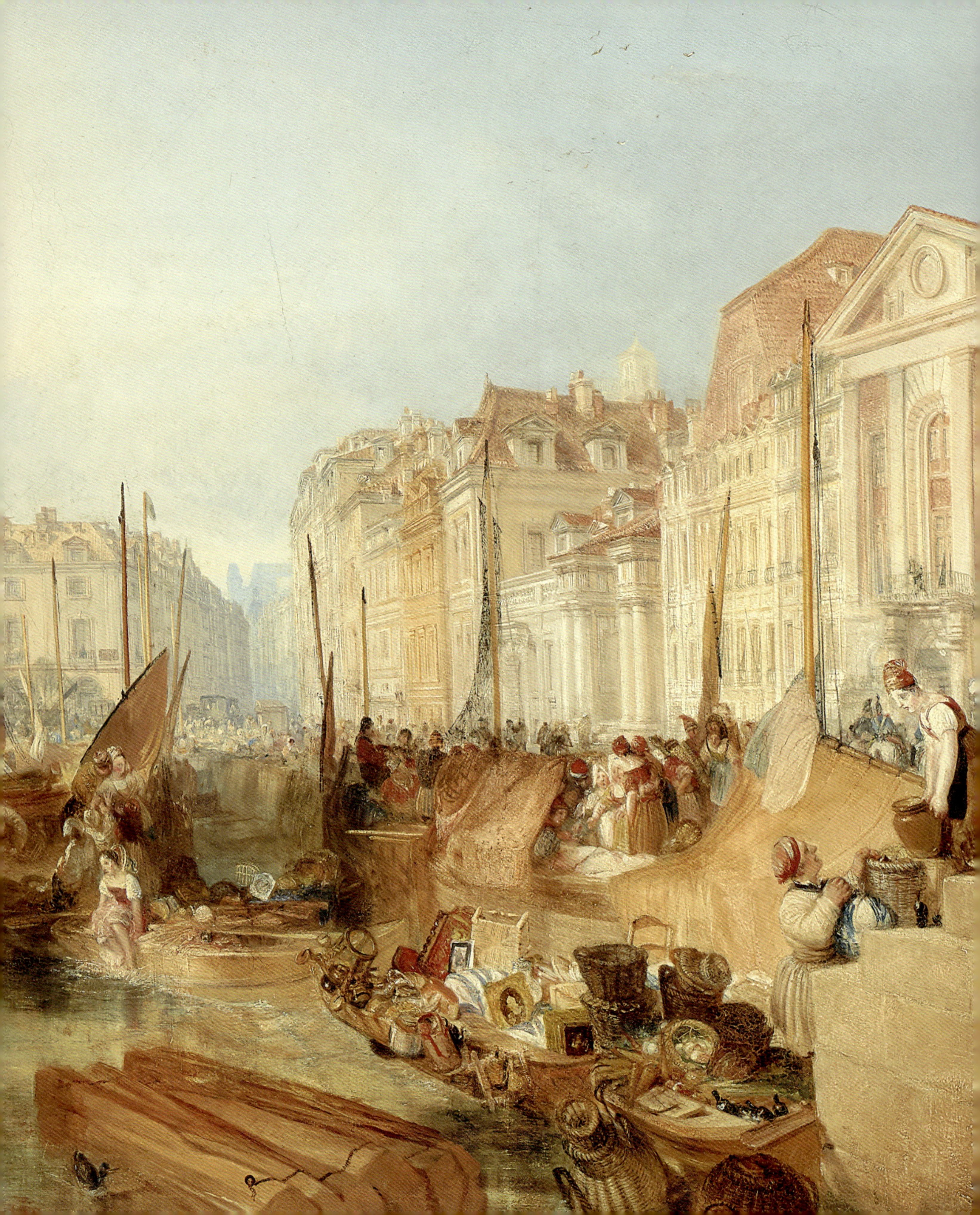

DIRECTORS' FOREWORD

Throughout his life J.M.W. Turner was an inveterate traveller in Britain and on the continent, and during his tours he produced thousands of sketches, some of which he would work up into the finished paintings he exhibited at the Royal Academy, London. By the mid-1820s, when he showed *Harbour of Dieppe: Changement de Domicile* (in 1825) and *Cologne, the Arrival of a Packet-Boat: Evening* (in 1826), two of his most ambitious canvases, he was Britain's most revered painter, admired for his atmospheric landscapes, seascapes and harbour scenes, with their vast sweep and astounding light effects. Turner had been seeking for some years to emulate, indeed to outdo, the achievements of the classicising French artist, Claude Lorrain, and the Dutch painters of the Golden Age, and these two works demonstrated how far he had advanced in his purpose.

A few years earlier, in 1824, the National Gallery had opened in a private house in Pall Mall with a display that included several paintings by Claude, which Turner had known and admired when they were owned by the financier and collector John Julius Angerstein. In his mind there began to develop the plan to donate his paintings to the nation and after his death the Gallery became the custodian of his vast legacy. Turner among the great European masters at the National Gallery, now in Trafalgar Square, offered an impressive spectacle that had a mesmerising effect on the wealthy American collectors of the Gilded Age, among them the industrialist Henry Clay Frick (1849–1919). He acquired the two great Turners of Dieppe and Cologne in 1914 and displayed them with his impressive collection of old masters in his new house on Fifth Avenue in New York, now The Frick Collection, moving in with his family at the end of the year.

A little more than a century later, as The Frick Collection buildings are being renovated and enhanced (under the direction of architect Annabelle Selldorf, who is also responsible for the National Gallery Bicentenary capital project, NG200), the two paintings are being lent to the National Gallery, marking the first time they have left the Frick's galleries and the first time they have been seen in Britain since 1911. We are delighted that the London public has been given the opportunity to enjoy these works and we want to express our enormous gratitude to the Trustees of The Frick Collection for making this possible. We are grateful to Christine Riding, Thomas Ardill and Aimee Ng for their contributions to this publication.

The exhibition is supported by the Capricorn Foundation, in memory of Mr H.J. Hyams, and we would like to express our gratitude to the Trustees for their continued support of the National Gallery.

GABRIELE FINALDI, DIRECTOR
The National Gallery, London

IAN WARDROPPER, DIRECTOR
The Frick Collection, New York

Detail of cat. 1

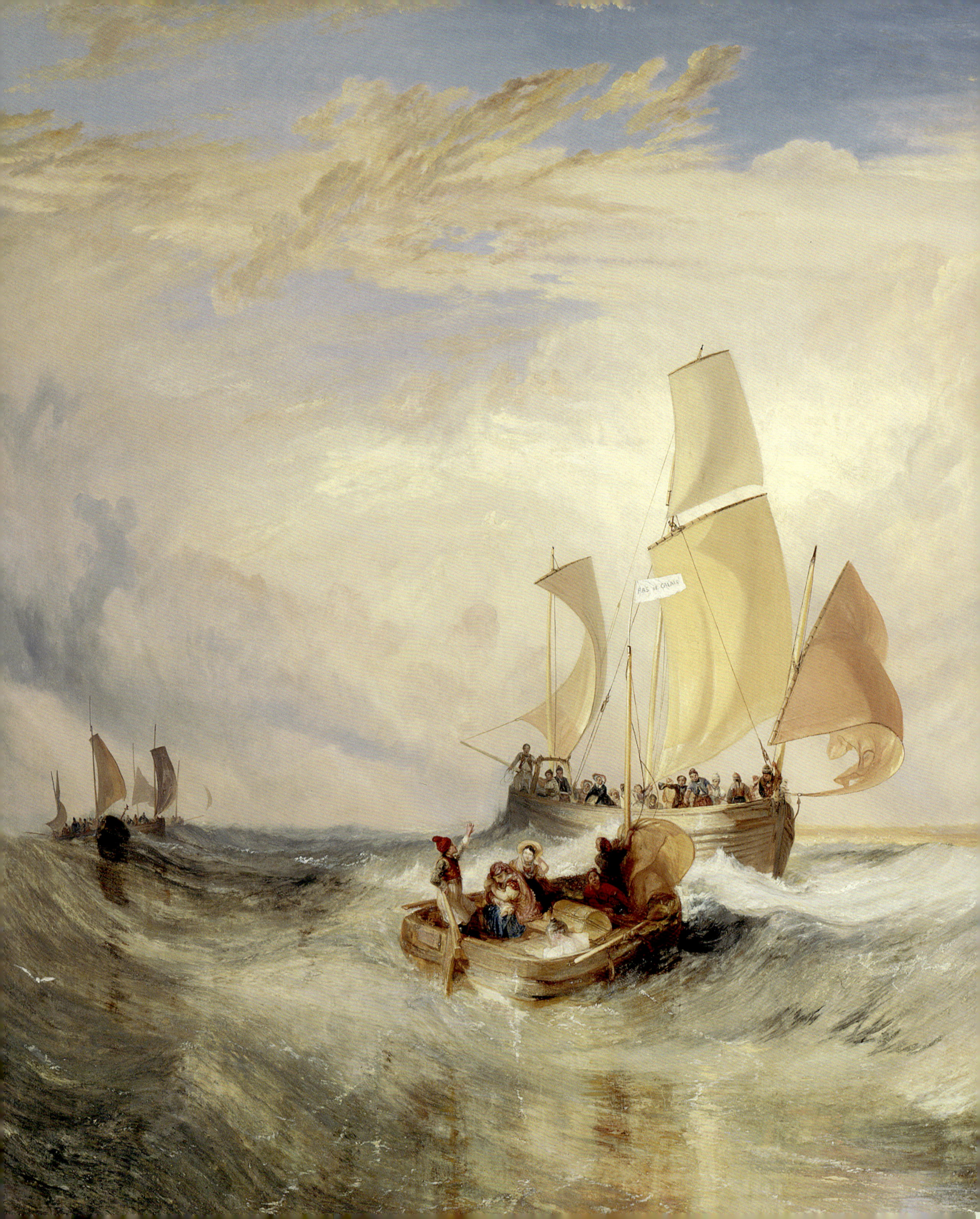
PAS DE CALAIS

JOURNEYS OLD AND NEW: TURNER IN THE 1820s

Christine Riding

Detail of fig. 8

In 1825, Joseph Mallord William (J.M.W.) Turner (1775–1851) showed one work at the Royal Academy's annual exhibition, a large, luminous oil painting entitled *Harbour of Dieppe: Changement de Domicile* (*Change of Home Address*, cat. 1). The following year, he submitted a closely related river scene, *Cologne, the Arrival of a Packet-Boat: Evening* (cat. 2). Such images of arrival and departure, of commerce and leisure, whether at domestic or foreign ports, quays and waterfronts, had been a regular feature of Turner's work, and this would continue for the rest of his career. Accordingly, *Dieppe* and *Cologne* represented a consistent artistic approach to maritime subjects and furthermore drew on Turner's usual practice of first-hand observation while travelling at home and abroad, in this case using material gathered during recent sketching tours to Europe. Likewise, these paintings demonstrated Turner's continuing engagement with a rich continental tradition, from seventeenth-century French classicism and eighteenth-century Italian *vedute* (topographical views) to Dutch coastal scenes and Western marine art, which favoured contemporary and quotidian subject matter. The latter was also intimately connected to the UK and other European naval and colonial powers.[1]

Despite such continuities, *Dieppe* and *Cologne* represented a significant departure for Turner, particularly in terms of colour and technique, the evidence of which was even more striking to his critics given that they were the first harbour scenes Turner had shown at the Royal Academy since 1818 (with *Dort or Dordrecht: The Dort Packet-Boat from Rotterdam becalmed*, fig. 1). At this stage in his career, Turner was a mature and commercially successful artist and esteemed Academician, largely unrivalled as the nation's pre-eminent

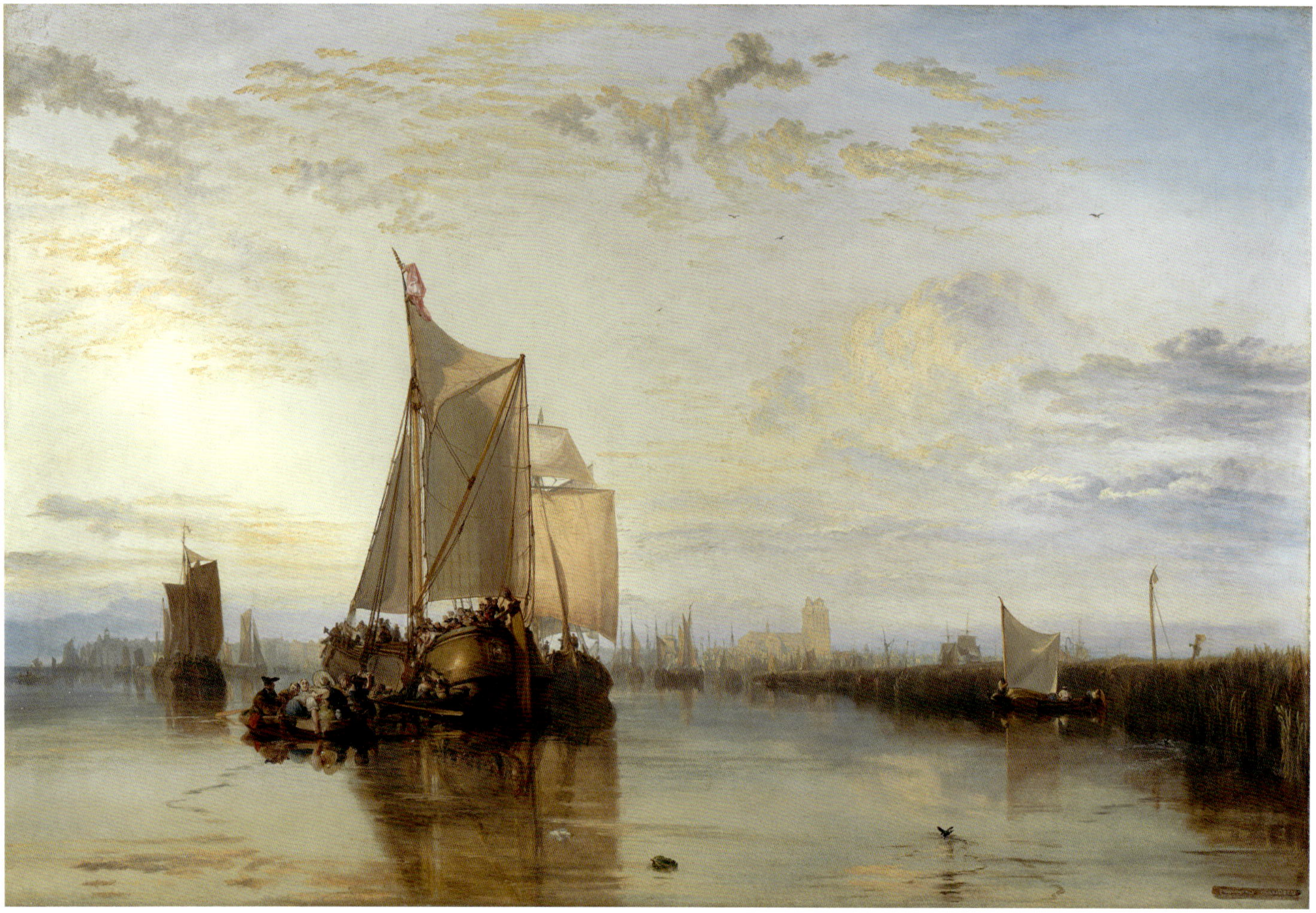

1 *Dort or Dordrecht: The Dort Packet-Boat from Rotterdam becalmed*, 1818, oil on canvas, 157.5 × 233.7 cm, Yale Center for British Art, Paul Mellon Collection, New Haven, Connecticut (B1977.14.77)

landscape painter in both oil and watercolour. Far from resting on his laurels, however, *Dieppe* and *Cologne* showed that he was prone to going his own way in matters of art, spurred by his habitual competitiveness towards his fellow artists and insatiable desire to go beyond, rather than simply repeat, his previous successes. Tellingly, these paintings came at a time when he had been exhibiting for some 30 years and, now in his fifties, was increasingly preoccupied with his own artistic legacy and place among the old masters. This was signalled by the terms set out in his will of 1829, which culminated (after numerous revisions) in a substantial bequest of autograph works to the national collection and provision for their public display after his death.

NAVIGATING A SEA CHANGE

Some measure of how far Turner was pushing the boundaries of artistic representation in the mid-1820s can be gleaned from the qualified praise and baffled criticism he received at the time, largely in response to his use of brilliant colour applied to real and contemporary (as opposed to imaginary or ideal) subjects. Of course, Turner was no stranger to controversy and had come under fire from conservative critics early in his career, especially from the influential connoisseur and patron Sir George Beaumont (1753–1827). Beaumont's oft-quoted critique of *Calais Pier* (1803, fig. 19), in which he described Turner's liberal use of opaque white

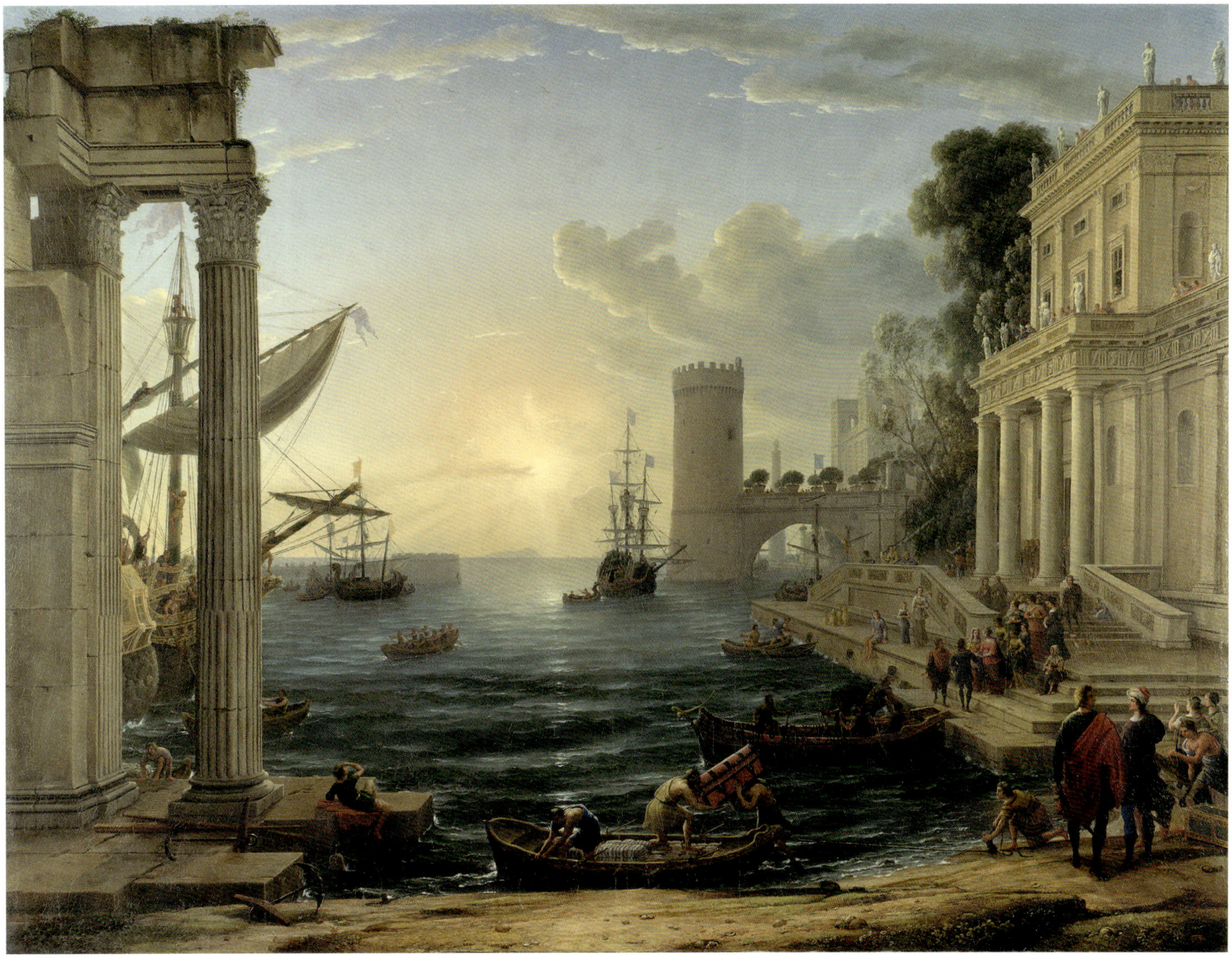

2 Claude (1604/5?–1682), *Seaport with the Embarkation of the Queen of Sheba*, 1648, oil on canvas, 149.1 × 196.7 cm, The National Gallery, London (NG14)

to suggest agitated water as looking 'like the veins on a marble Slab', mainly hinged on the artist's flagrant disregard (as Beaumont saw it) of the old master tradition.[2] At the same time, Beaumont and others promoted a hierarchy within the tradition itself, with the 'ideal' of the classicist principles – represented by seventeenth-century French painters Claude Lorrain (born Claude Gellée, known as Claude, 1604/5?–1682) and Gaspard Dughet (1615–1675), both based in Rome, and the Neapolitan Salvator Rosa (1615–1673) – taking precedence over the 'lowly' naturalism and modern-day subject matter typical of Dutch landscapes, exemplified by Willem van de Velde the Younger (1633–1707) and Aelbert Cuyp (1620–1691).

Of all these artists, Claude was seen as the model of refinement, epitomising classical beauty through the formal harmony and subtle luminosity of his landscapes and seaports, elevated into the more prestigious genre of history painting by the inclusion of classical architecture and figures alluding to scenes from the Bible or classical mythology. By the end of the eighteenth century, Claude's status in the UK was unsurpassed among collectors and connoisseurs, many of whom had encountered his work in royal and aristocratic collections in Paris and Rome while on the Grand Tour. Following the French Revolution of 1789 and Napoleon's invasions of Italy between 1796 and 1801, many more paintings by Claude reached the London art market and consequently entered British private collections. These included *Seaport with the Embarkation of the Queen of Sheba* (fig. 2) and *Landscape with the Marriage of Isaac and Rebekah ('The Mill')* (1648, National Gallery, London), both made for Frédéric-Maurice, Duc de Bouillon (1605–1652), a French general in the papal army in Rome, and acquired in 1803 by John Julius Angerstein (1735–1823), a financier and collector.[3]

From the beginning of his career, Turner engaged with both Dutch and French traditions. One of his earliest paintings, *Dutch Boats in a Gale* (private collection), was commissioned in 1801 as a companion to a seascape by Van de Velde, *Ships in a Stormy Sea* (1671–2, Toledo Museum of Art), in the collection of the 3rd Duke of Bridgewater. By drawing direct parallels in this way between past and present, Turner and his contemporaries clearly had one eye on the art market, as well as taking advantage of the greater access to original artworks now on their doorstep. Turner's much-admired *Dort* was modelled on *The Maas at Dordrecht* (about 1650, National Gallery of Art, Washington, DC) by Cuyp, a work acquired in 1815 by Sir Abraham Hume (1749–1838), who, along with Beaumont, was a founding member of the British Institution, and in the same year, the painting itself was included in the old masters exhibition held there. Often referred to as 'the Dutch Claude', Cuyp painted tranquil harbour scenes that were among the most sought-after paintings of the time. It was undoubtedly this assimilation of Claudian effects and motifs, alongside the rugged landscapes of Dughet and Rosa, that explains the lasting appeal in the UK of the harbour and coastal views by Frenchman Claude-Joseph Vernet (1714–1789), an artist to whom Turner made direct reference (alongside another eighteenth-century master of moonlit scenes, Joseph Wright of Derby [1734–1797]) in his first exhibited oil painting, *Fishermen at Sea* (1796, Tate, London).[4]

Turner's admiration for Claude would last his entire career. The French artist's influence can be seen in such early works as *Sun rising through Vapour: Fishermen cleaning and selling Fish* (before 1807, National Gallery, London) and Turner's ambitious print project *Liber Studiorum* (Book of Studies), begun in about 1806 as a kind of homage to Claude's celebrated *Liber Veritatis* (Book of Truth, begun in 1635/6), but it was not until 1815 that Turner created an oil painting, *Dido building Carthage* (National Gallery, London), that deliberately set out to match Claude's seaport paintings, both formally and thematically. *The Decline of the Carthaginian Empire* (Tate, London) followed in 1817, which led one critic at the Royal Academy to proclaim that 'Mr Turner has only one [painting in the exhibition], but that one is a lion … excelling in the higher qualities of art, mind and poetical conception, even Claude himself.'[5]

Consequently, Turner's rationale in exhibiting an ambitious harbour scene like *Dieppe*, after an interval of some seven years, may well be connected to the acquisition in 1824 of three imaginary seaports by Claude, including the previously mentioned *Embarkation of the Queen of Sheba*, for the newly founded National Gallery, along with other masterpieces from the prestigious Angerstein collection. According to an apocryphal story, the 'very young Turner' had wept before one of these seaports, overwhelmed by Claude's achievement and the impossibility of him matching it, let alone challenging it.[6] Whether it is true or not, this anecdote neatly underscores that Claude functioned as a touchstone for Turner in terms of his own progress as a painter. It may also explain the bolder luminosity of *Dieppe*, *Cologne* and other paintings of this period. Indeed, it was not the use of classical or biblical motifs and narratives that distinguished Claude from other old masters but the painterly effect, at once indefinable and yet distinctive, that he managed to achieve in his paintings: 'a brilliancy', to quote an admirer in 1812, 'so happily blended and subdued by an almost visible atmosphere, that the whole is splendour, the whole is repose'.[7] On viewing *Dieppe*, for example, a commentator in the *European Magazine* concluded that not even Claude 'has exceeded the brilliant composition before us: in transparent effect it is equal to that great master; while in the drawing and grouping of numerous figures, it is superior'.[8] Meanwhile, in the opinion of the *Literary Magnet* reviewer, 'Mr Turner's brilliant experiment upon colours … displays all the magic of skill at the expense of all the magic of nature,' a sentiment repeated in other publications.[9]

What provoked the more ambivalent comments was not simply the heightened register of colour – particularly the use of yellow, which struck some as 'unnatural' – but also that the modern context or existent subject made it additionally incongruous and, as a result, inappropriate. The diarist Henry Crabb Robinson (1775–1867), while acknowledging that the painting was 'magnificent', posed the question, if Turner 'will invest an atmosphere, and a play of colours all his own, why will he not assume a romantic name?' 'No one', Robinson continued, 'could find fault with a Garden of Armida, or even of Eden, so painted. But we know Dieppe, in the north of France, and can't easily clothe it in such fairy hues.'[10]

The technical innovations with which Robinson and others were grappling were chiefly the result of recent and related developments in Turner's career: his extended travels on the continent, and his more profound engagement with the creative and commercial opportunities afforded by the medium of watercolour. For most of Turner's adult life up to the age of 40, Great Britain (from 1801, the UK) and its allies were embroiled in the French Revolutionary and Napoleonic Wars (1792–1815), making foreign travel practically impossible. Consequently, all but one of Turner's sketching tours before hostilities ceased were conducted within the UK. But these regular trips would increasingly align with arguably the most significant development for Turner at the time: his participation in numerous commercial print projects involving a series of topographical views, financed primarily by professional engravers and publishers. These initiatives reflected a broader trend in the print market for specifically British subjects and the related growth in domestic tourism stimulated from the late eighteenth century by the fashionable idea of the 'picturesque tour'.[11] Starting with *Picturesque Views on the Southern Coast of England* (1814–26), a steady stream of projects emerged, all of which contained harbours and/or riverfronts by Turner, including *The Provincial Antiquities and Picturesque Scenery of Scotland* (about 1822–5), *The Rivers of England* (1822–6), *Marine Views* (about 1817–24) and, coinciding with the exhibition of his *Dieppe* and *Cologne* paintings, *The Ports of England* (1825–8).[12] While Turner used his substantial creative powers on these projects, the crucial point here is that he was representing actual places in modern times, the very antithesis in fact of the ideal and the imaginary. Furthermore, the unprecedented breadth and quality of the watercolours he made resulted in Turner achieving an unrivalled reputation at home and subsequently abroad.

With peace declared in 1815, Turner made trips to France, Germany and the Low Countries, and then, in August 1819, he left England for his long-awaited tour of Italy. Over the course of six months he stayed in Rome, Venice and other towns and cities, immersing himself in the colour and light of the surrounding countryside, particularly the Roman Campagna. For Turner and his fellow landscape artists, to journey to Italy was to follow in the footsteps of Claude. On returning to London, Turner chose to exhibit oils at the Royal Academy that were predominantly classicising landscapes, such as *Rome, from the Vatican* of 1820, and three years later, *The Bay of Baiae, with Apollo and the Sibyl* (both Tate, London), perhaps with the intention of emphasising the profound influence Italy had had on his art. Interestingly, the former painting

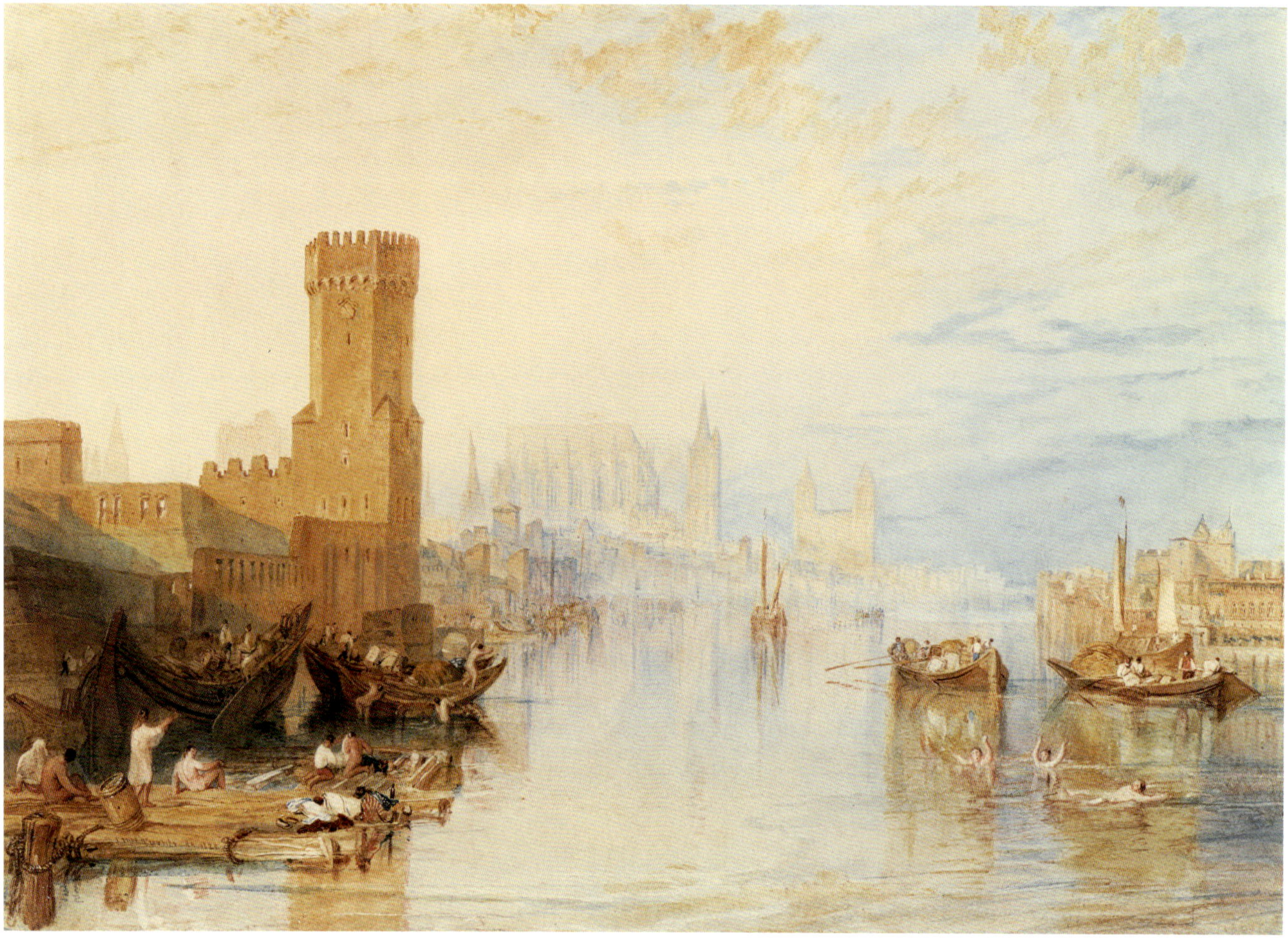

3 *Cologne from the River*, 1820, watercolour on paper, 30.8 × 46.3 cm, Seattle Art Museum, Washington. Gift of Mr and Mrs Louis Brechemin (70.70)

was simultaneously praised for its 'richness and splendour of colouring' and condemned for its 'excessive yellowness'.[13]

This focus on Italy partly explains the lack of large-scale modern harbour scenes and other marine paintings during the early 1820s. However, when it came to sketching tours and finished watercolours, Turner was anything but inactive on the topic, his artistic endeavours now extending to topographical views in Europe. Hence, he gathered material in Dieppe during a trip to Normandy in 1821 (cat. 1.2) and visited the French fishing port on two further occasions before painting the *Dieppe* canvas in his London studio.[14] In the case of the *Cologne* painting, Turner made sketches during a visit to the town in the autumn of 1817 (fig. 14) and again in September 1825 (cat. 2.2).[15] In 1820, he created a highly finished watercolour showing Cologne's famous waterfront from the south (fig. 3), the opposite orientation from that of the painting made six years later (cat. 2). The intense colour tones and translucency of this and other watercolours resulted directly from Turner's experimentation with the medium. And it was precisely these artistic insights that he transferred to his exhibited work in oil.

FELLOW TRAVELLERS

In addition to his involvement with print culture, Turner's work in watercolour reached wider audiences through a succession of

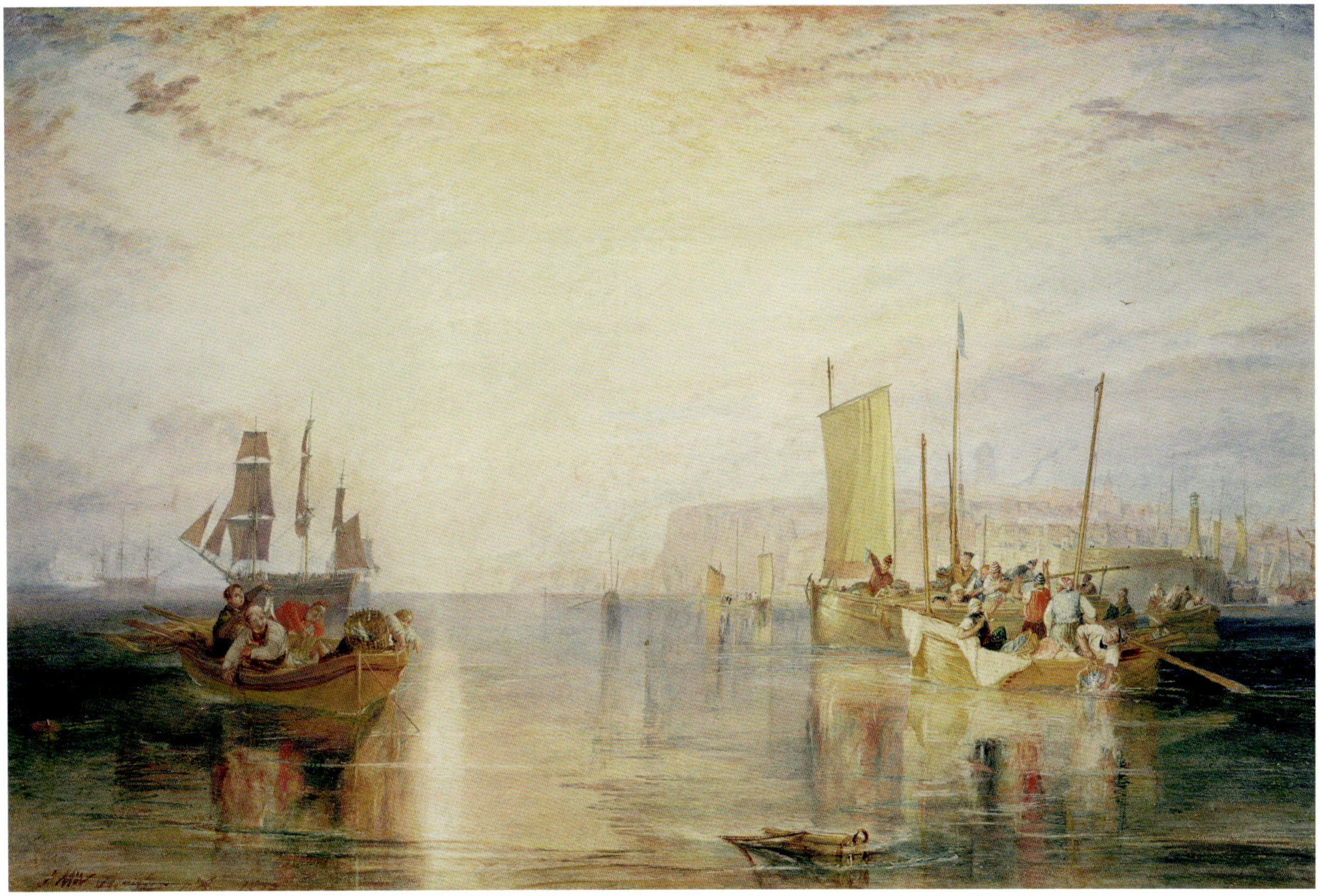

4 *Sun-Rise: Whiting fishing at Margate*, 1822, watercolour on paper, 42.6 × 64.8 cm, private collection

London exhibitions. In 1819, more than 60 of his watercolours were displayed at the residence of his friend and patron Walter Fawkes (1769–1825), who had purchased *Dort* in 1818; and during the 1820s and 1830s, Turner gave his permission for numerous exhibitions in commercial premises. From February to August 1822, the engraver-publisher William Bernard Cooke (1778–1855) staged one in Soho Square with more than 20 of Turner's watercolours, and this was followed by shows in 1823 and 1824, the former including *Dover Castle from the Sea* (1822, Museum of Fine Arts, Boston) and *Sun-Rise: Whiting fishing at Margate* (fig. 4) from the *Marine Views* series. Turner's depiction of Margate, a coastal town he had known since childhood, reveals the extent to which he was deftly using the greater portability of watercolour (in comparison to oil), combined with the freedom and speed of execution characteristic of the medium, while exploiting the full range of colours – intense greens, vibrant blues and, most of all, chrome yellows – that had become available via specialist merchants. The techniques employed here, to capture a radiant sunrise, reflections on water, and a distant cliff and town, were imitated in *Dieppe*, *Cologne* and other paintings from the 1820s by the application of thin layers of paint and translucent glazes – a marked departure from the highly textured surfaces of his early paintings, such as *Calais Pier* (fig. 19) and *Fishing Boats entering Calais Harbour* (about 1803, The Frick Collection). That Turner would continue to explore the creative interrelationship between the two mediums is

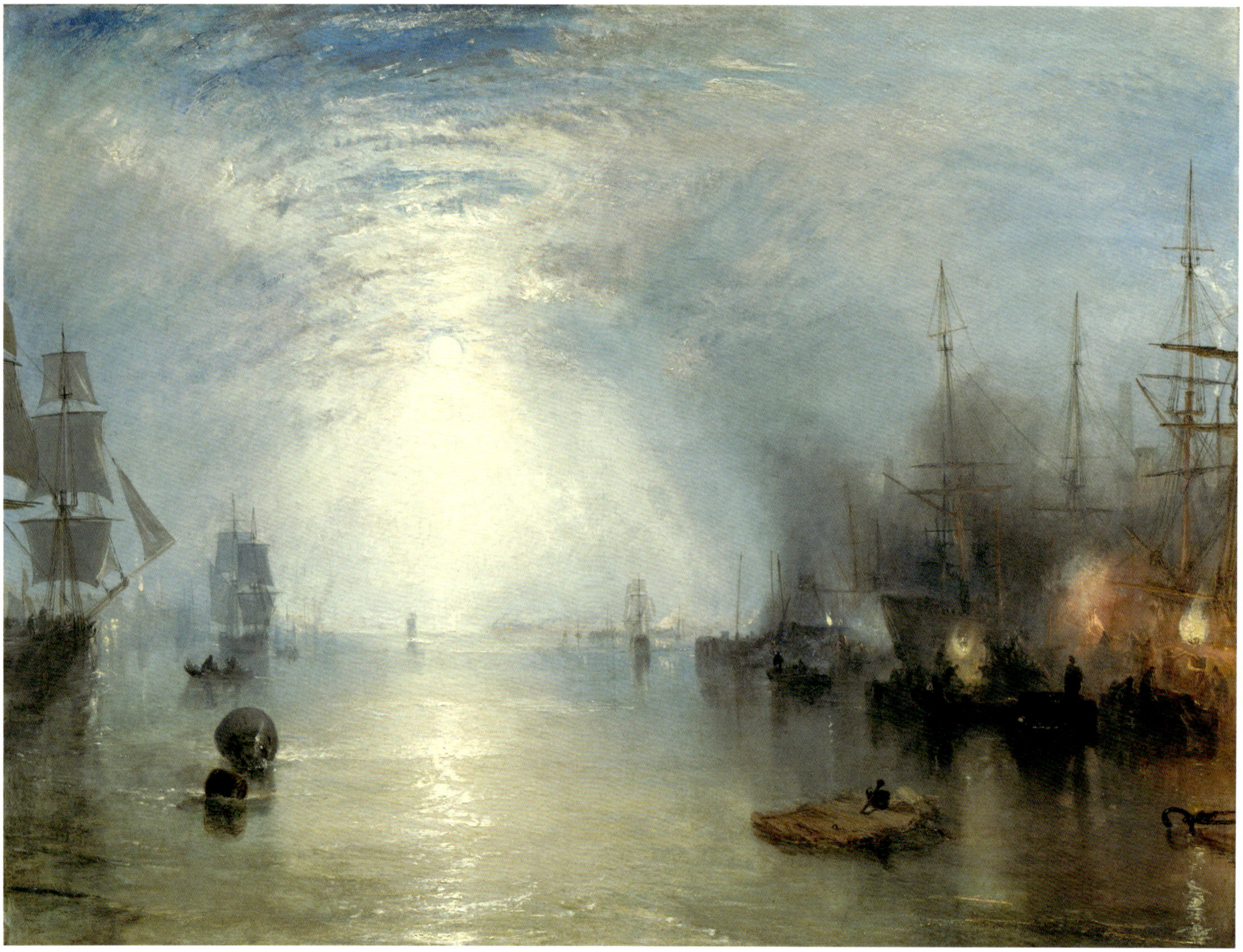

5 *Keelmen heaving in Coals by Moonlight*, 1835, oil on canvas, 92.3 × 122.8 cm, National Gallery of Art, Washington, DC, Widener Collection (1942.9.86)

clearly shown by the watercolour *Shields, on the River Tyne* (1823, Tate, London), made for the *Rivers of England* series, being reworked and transformed into a shimmeringly poetic oil painting, *Keelmen heaving in Coals by Moonlight* (fig. 5), shown at the Royal Academy in 1835.

During the 1820s, it was increasingly apparent that Turner's paintings stood some distance from those of other artists, particularly his exact contemporaries Augustus Wall Callcott (1779–1844) and John Constable (1776–1837). One need only think of the striking contrast between Constable's *The Leaping Horse* (1825, Royal Academy, London) and *The Cornfield* (1826, National Gallery, London) and Turner's *Dieppe* and *Cologne*, at the same Royal Academy exhibitions. But this had not always been the case. In the previous decade, Callcott had become a serious challenger to Turner in creating large-scale river and harbour scenes in the Dutch style. Indeed, his magnificent *Entrance to the Pool of London* of 1816 (Bowood House, Wiltshire), commissioned by the 3rd Marquess of Lansdowne, transformed Cuyp's *Maas at Dordrecht* into a contemporary Thames view. Greatly admired, it strengthened the opinion of many in the art world that Callcott and Turner were equals as marine painters. Hence Turner's

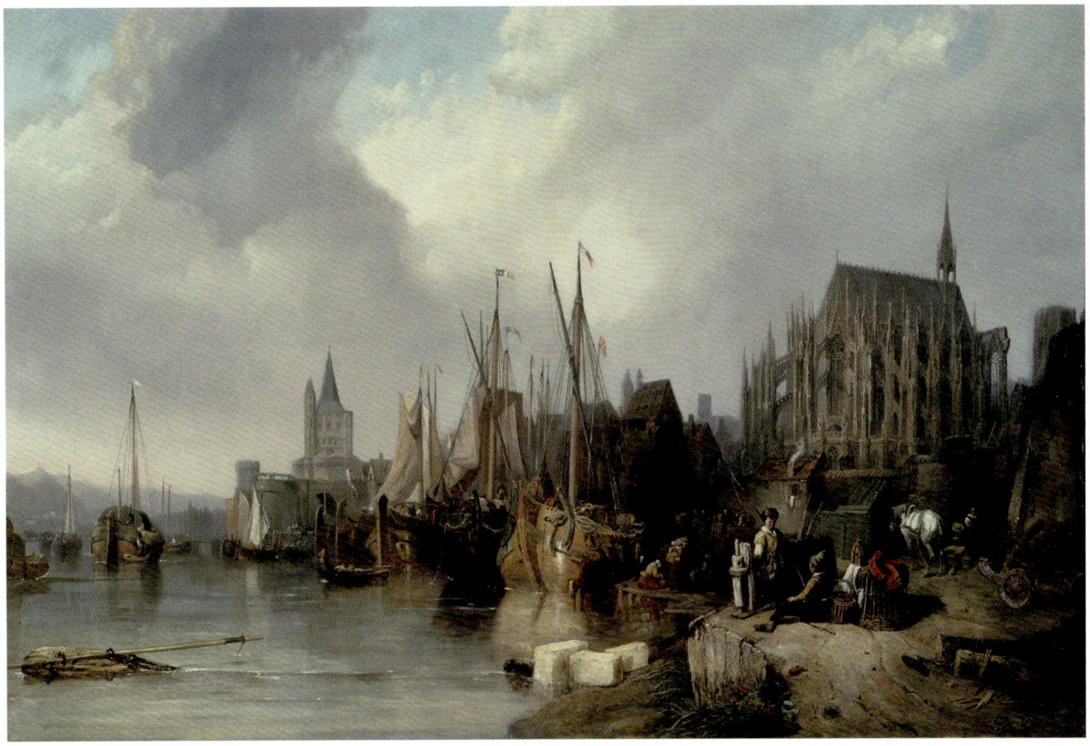

6 Clarkson Stanfield (1793–1867), *The Banks of the Rhine in Cologne with the Unfinished Cathedral*, about 1826, oil on canvas, 113 × 168 cm, Rheinisches Landesmuseum, Bonn

Dort, painted two years later, was as much a response to a contemporary rival as to an esteemed old master. For the rest of his career, however, Callcott continued to produce works, such as *The Quay at Antwerp during the Fair Time* (1826, Woburn Abbey, Bedfordshire), that broadly followed the tried and tested formula of his previous successes, thus appealing, as time went on, to more conservative tastes.

If Turner's immediate peers remained largely unaffected by his current innovations, this was not true of younger painters such as William Collins (1788–1847), Clarkson Stanfield (1793–1867) and Richard Parkes Bonington (1802–1828), for whom Turner was both a model and a rival. By the late 1810s Collins had a following among British collectors for his rural and coastal scenes, and after a visit to Paris in 1817 he began to paint French subjects in a similar vein, two of which were included at the Royal Academy in 1825. Likewise spurred by the renewed interest in foreign landscapes and topographical views, Stanfield (who at the time was employed as a scene painter at Drury Lane) travelled to Belgium and Germany in 1823 and 1824. As trips to the continent were relatively costly undertakings, it is likely that Stanfield's intention was to emulate Turner's growing reputation as an artist-traveller, as well as imbue his own paintings with the authority that travel itself was thought to bring about through direct experience and observation. Interestingly, Stanfield's *The Banks of the Rhine in Cologne* (fig. 6), more aesthetically aligned with Callcott than Turner at the time, was on exhibition at the Society of British Artists in 1826 while Turner's *Cologne* was at the Royal Academy. The same year, Bonington exhibited in London for the first time. English by birth, as a teenager he had moved to France with his family, and as a result he was a vital bridge between French and British art in the 1820s through his early focus on watercolour (little practised in France at the time) and his association with Eugène Delacroix (1798–1863), who was poised to become the leader of French Romantic art. Bonington had

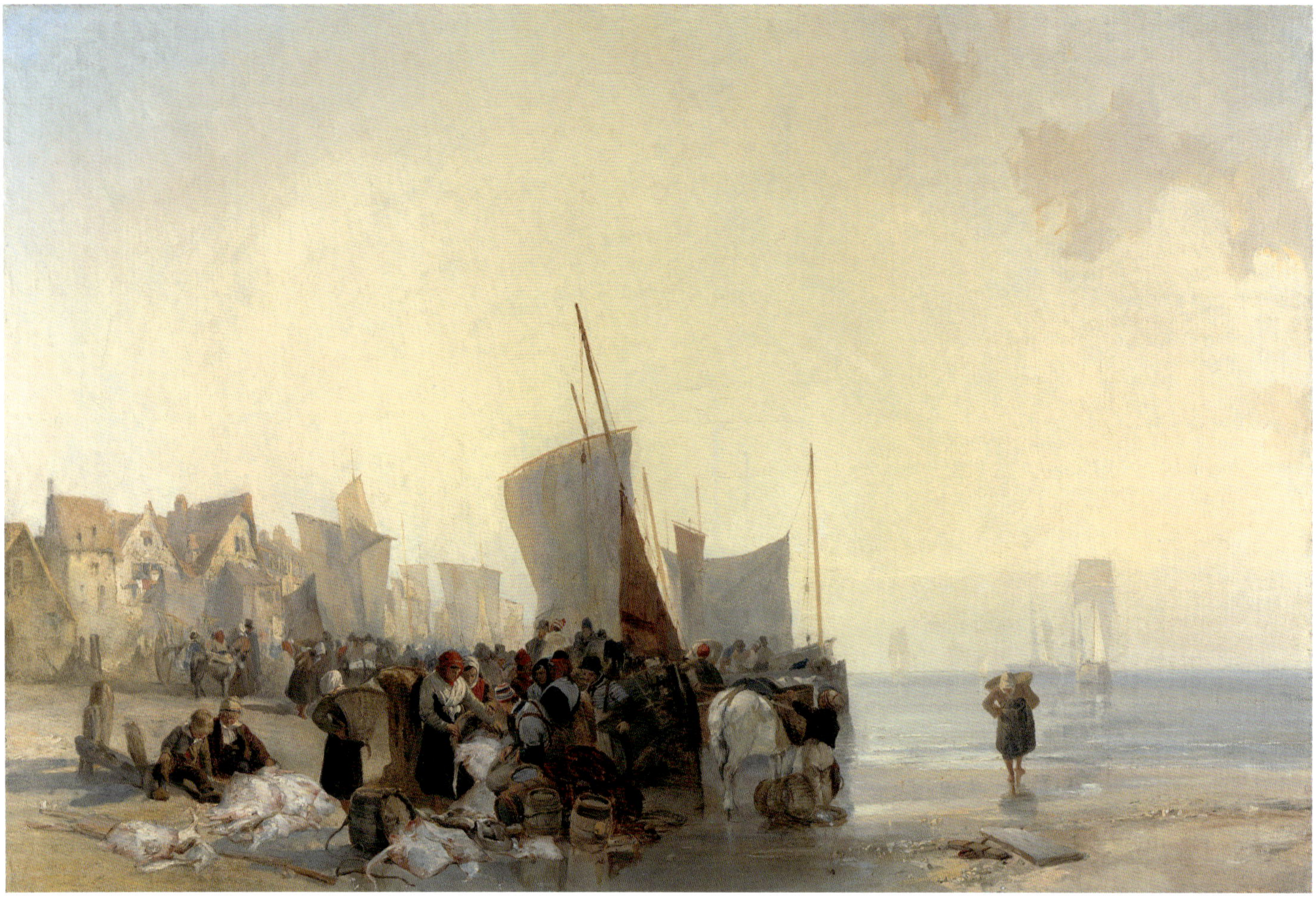

7 Richard Parkes Bonington (1802–1828), *A Fish-Market near Boulogne*, 1824, oil on canvas, 82.2 × 122.6 cm, Yale Center for British Art, Paul Mellon Collection, New Haven, Connecticut (B1981.25.50)

already caused a sensation at the Paris Salon in 1824 with *A Fish-Market near Boulogne* (fig. 7), his most ambitious marine painting, appearing alongside Constable's *Hay Wain* (1821, National Gallery, London) and *View on the Stour near Dedham* (1822, Huntington Art Collections, San Marino, California); both artists were awarded a gold medal by King Charles X. The breathtaking luminosity of Bonington's painting suggests, at the very least, a correlation with Turner's approach, although at this stage he likely knew the older artist's work only through engravings.

Perhaps surprisingly, Turner was not among the British artists who exhibited in Paris that year, nor at the other English Salon (Salon des Anglais) of 1826/7, which included Constable's *Cornfield* and Sir Thomas Lawrence's (1769–1830) portrait of Charles William Lambton (1825, National Gallery, London), now popularly known as *The Red Boy*.[16] Feasibly, his attention was focused elsewhere, not least on the potential for royal patronage. This in part explains his journey by sea to Edinburgh in 1822, which coincided with George IV's visit there (the artist was planning a series of works commemorating the royal event), and he multitasked by gathering material while travelling for the *Provincial Antiquities* and *Ports of England* series. Two years later, Turner's monumental canvas *The Battle of Trafalgar, 21 October 1805* (1822–4, National Maritime Museum, London), his only royal commission and the largest work he ever completed, was installed at St James's Palace. Even so, it was only a matter of time before

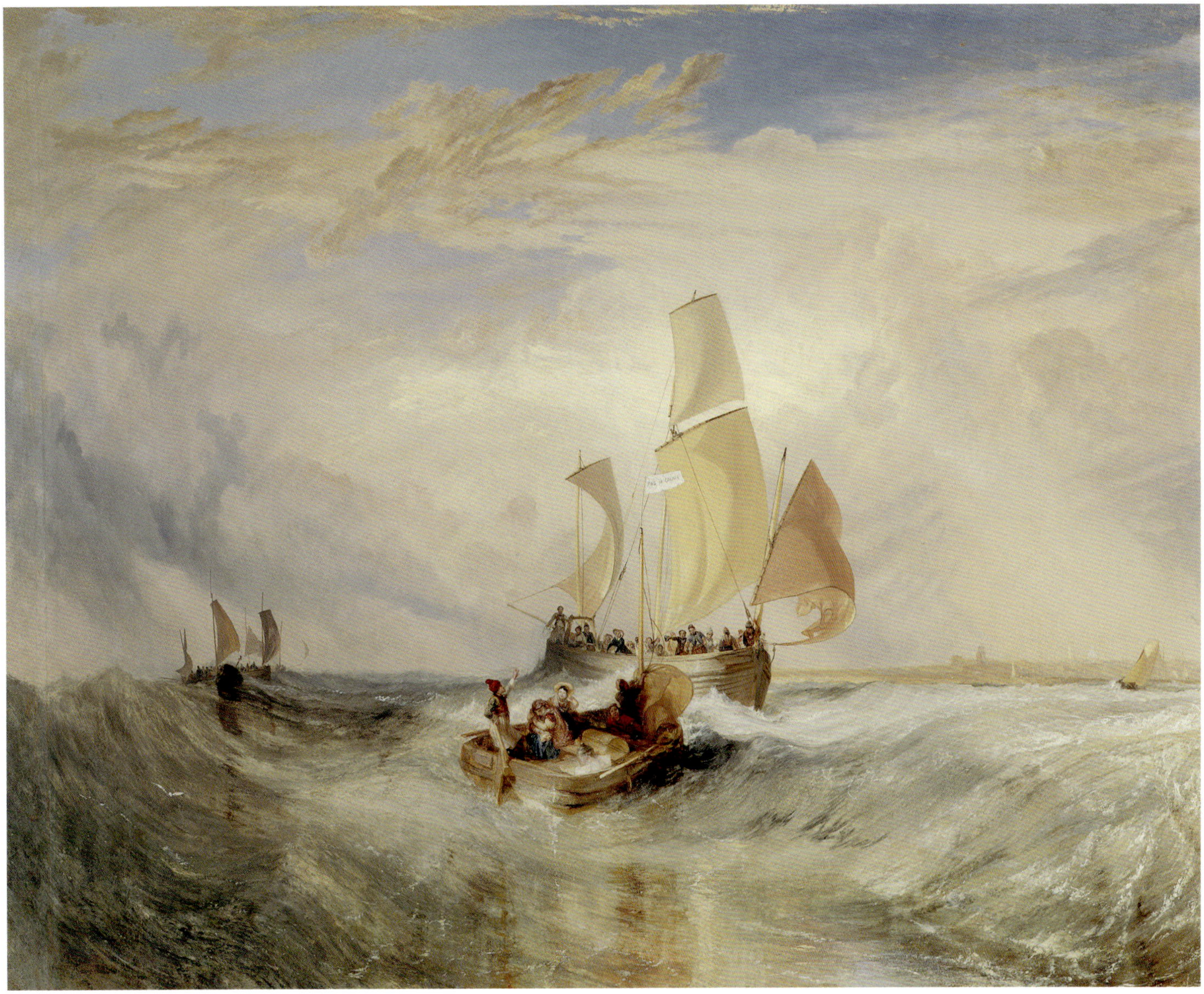

8 *'Now for the Painter' (Rope) – Passengers going on Board*, 1827, oil on canvas, 174.3 × 223.5 cm, Manchester Art Gallery, Manchester (1947.507)

Bonington presented a serious challenge to Turner on home ground. In the summer of 1825, visiting London along with Delacroix and other French artists, he saw Turner's work in oil and watercolour, including *Dieppe* and *Sun-Rise: Whiting fishing at Margate*. Under Turner's influence, Bonington's watercolour technique became more experimental and richly coloured. The following year, having noted the prevailing taste for coastal paintings by Turner, Collins and others, Bonington submitted two French scenes to the British Institution. These were bought immediately by two of its governors, the Marquess of Lansdowne and the Earl Grosvenor, prompting numerous commissions from other influential patrons.

After the success of his London debut, Bonington exhibited again in 1827, this time at the Royal Academy, with a French coastal scene owned by the Duke of Bedford. The exhibition itself was a watershed moment in British marine painting. Constable, whose seascapes and coastal scenes date from the mid-1820s, exhibited his first large-scale marine painting,

Chain Pier, Brighton (1826–7, Tate, London), as a response to market trends and to advance his hopes of being elected a full Academician. But he was also moving into territory long occupied by other painters, as his friend John Fisher noted at the time when he wrote to Constable's wife, Maria, 'Turner, Calcott [sic] and Collins will not like it.'[17] Indeed, Callcott, who tended to show one painting per year, submitted four in 1827, all coastal and river views, including *Bruges, from the Ghent Canal* (1827, location unknown), a marine townscape in the Dutch manner. Turner himself exhibited *'Now for the Painter' (Rope) – Passengers going on Board* (fig. 8), which shows travellers departing from Calais, and the brooding seascape *Port Ruysdael* (1826–7, Yale Center for British Art, New Haven), the fictive title alluding to Jacob van Ruisdael (1628/9?–1682) and underscoring Turner's continuing allegiance to Dutch marine painting.[18] *'Now for the Painter'* was reputedly titled in friendly rivalry with Stanfield, who had failed to complete a painting entitled *Throwing the Painter* in time for the 1826 exhibition (consequently, Callcott had extended the title of his own painting that year to read *Dutch Boats running Foul in the Endeavour to Board, and missing the Painter Rope*). The play on nautical terminology ('painter' being a rope used to tow or tie up a boat) with artistic identity, specifically the artist as seaborne traveller, suggests that Turner's title could also have been aimed at the young and old pretenders Bonington and Constable, the latter having never journeyed abroad. Furthermore, *'Now for the Painter'* relates, in scale, subject and painterly effects, to *Dieppe* and *Cologne*, so proclaiming (as the title suggests) Turner's own direction of travel.

TURNER'S ODYSSEY

Published reviews of *'Now for the Painter'* varied. Some critics admired it, some were hostile and others, despite their reservations, attempted to understand the artist's rationale: one thought the painting displayed 'much of the ultra both in effect and colour' but conceded that this arose 'from an exuberance of imagination; and there is "method in the madness"'.[19] The following year, Turner submitted a classical harbour scene, *Dido directing the Equipment of the Fleet, or the Morning of the Carthaginian Empire* (1828, Tate, London), and two luminous contemporary views inspired by East Cowes Regatta to the Royal Academy, once more provoking mixed reviews.[20] In the autumn, he travelled again to Italy, arriving in Rome by October (Bonington had died the previous month, aged just 25). For one week in December he exhibited some newly finished oils, *Vision of Medea* (1828), *View of Orvieto* (1828, reworked 1830) and *Regulus* (fig. 9; all Tate, London), at his lodgings. Given the association between Rome and Claude, it was plainly strategic that both *Orvieto* and *Regulus* were variations on the old master's signature landscapes and seaports. But there, perhaps equally deliberately, the comparison ends. Turner's fellow artist Charles Eastlake (1793–1865) observed that more than one thousand people visited the exhibition and 'how astonished, enraged or delighted the different schools of artists were, at seeing things so new, so daring and excellencies so unequivocal'.[21] Of course, only those who had visited London would have witnessed at first hand the evolution of Turner's work in oil, perhaps explaining the strength of feeling described by Eastlake.

As a classical seaport, *Regulus* highlights how Turner continually used this quintessential 'old master' theme to measure his own artistic development, and how he effortlessly moved between representations of the ancient (ideal) and the modern (actual). In doing so, Turner explored not only the classicist tradition in art but also, by extension, the allusive relationship between past and present imperial and maritime powers, from Carthage, Rome and Venice to France and the UK, often reflecting on the idea, engrained in European culture, that all nations rise and fall.[22] Turner's first exhibited seaports in the Claudian manner, discussed above, represented the ascendancy and the decline of

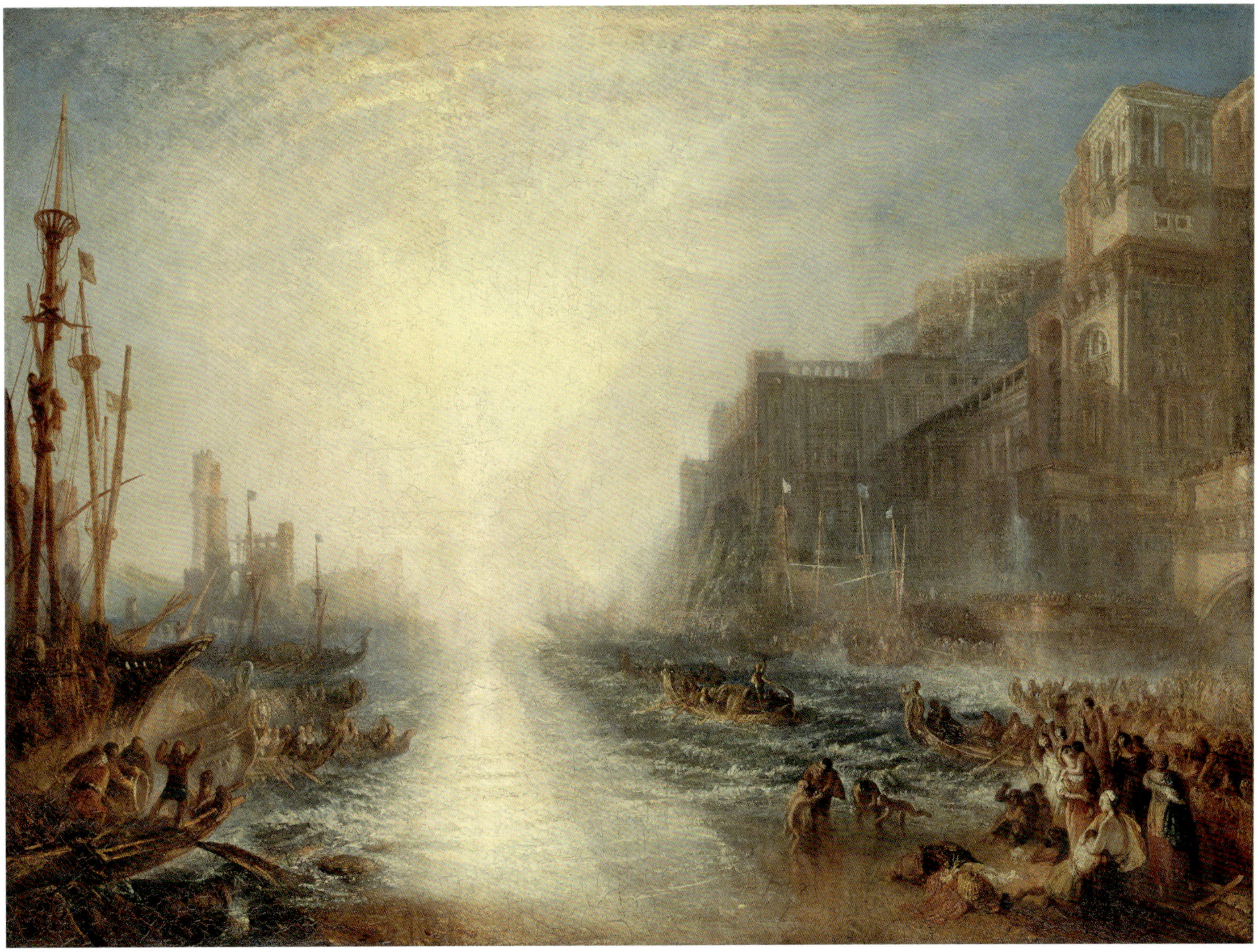

9 *Regulus*, 1828, reworked 1837, oil on canvas, 89.5 × 123.8 cm, Tate, London (N00519)

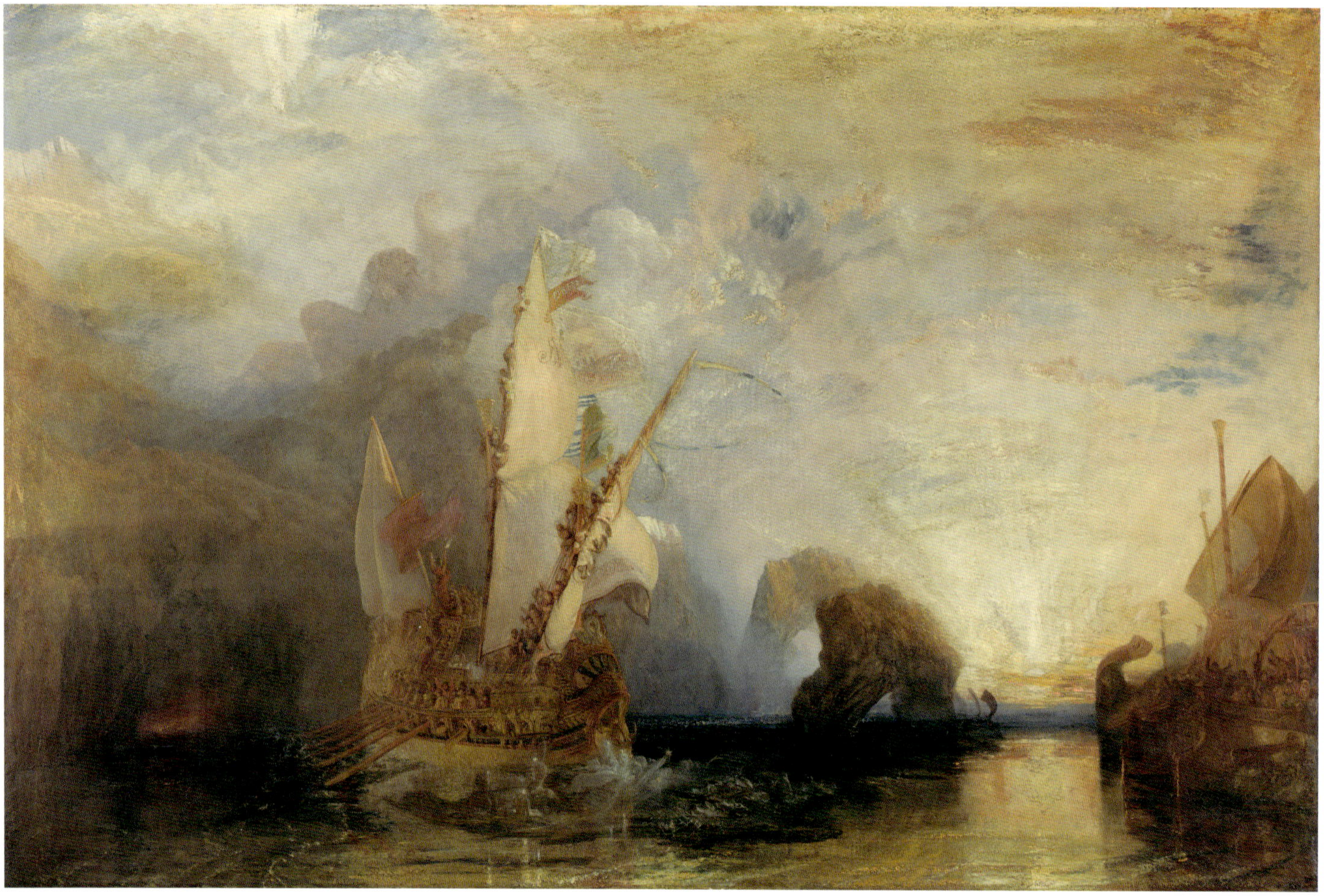

10 *Ulysses deriding Polyphemus – Homer's Odyssey*, 1829, oil on canvas, 132.5 × 203 cm, The National Gallery, London (NG508)

Carthage, symbolised by the rising and setting of the sun. Regulus was the Roman general whom the Carthaginians blinded by removing his eyelids and placing him in direct sunlight. Thus, the spectator of Turner's dazzling canvas stands in for Regulus himself. The story surely resonated personally with Turner at the time, not least in reflecting comments expressed by his detractors. Only months before, one critic had warned exhibition visitors (in response to *Morning of the Carthaginian Empire*) to 'veil your sight … or it will be over-powered by the glare of the violent colours assembled'.[23] Turner developed this theme still further in his now-celebrated *Ulysses deriding Polyphemus – Homer's Odyssey* (fig. 10), which was exhibited at the Royal Academy in 1829. Turner shows Ulysses setting sail into a fiery sunrise, away from the island where Polyphemus, a cyclops (one-eyed giant) and son of Poseidon, god of the sea, had held him captive. The escape was made possible by Ulysses blinding Polyphemus as he slept. Alluding to this moment, one critic quipped, 'That is really no reason why Mr Turner should put out the eyes of us, harmless critics.' Others, however, judged the painting to be a 'gorgeous vision of the imagination' and full of 'poetical feeling'.[24]

The leading American landscape artist Thomas Cole (1801–1848) visited London in 1829. He went to the National Gallery (then located on Pall Mall), where he paid close attention to Claude's paintings, and to the Royal Academy exhibition, making sketches with colour notes of *Ulysses deriding Polyphemus*, observing its

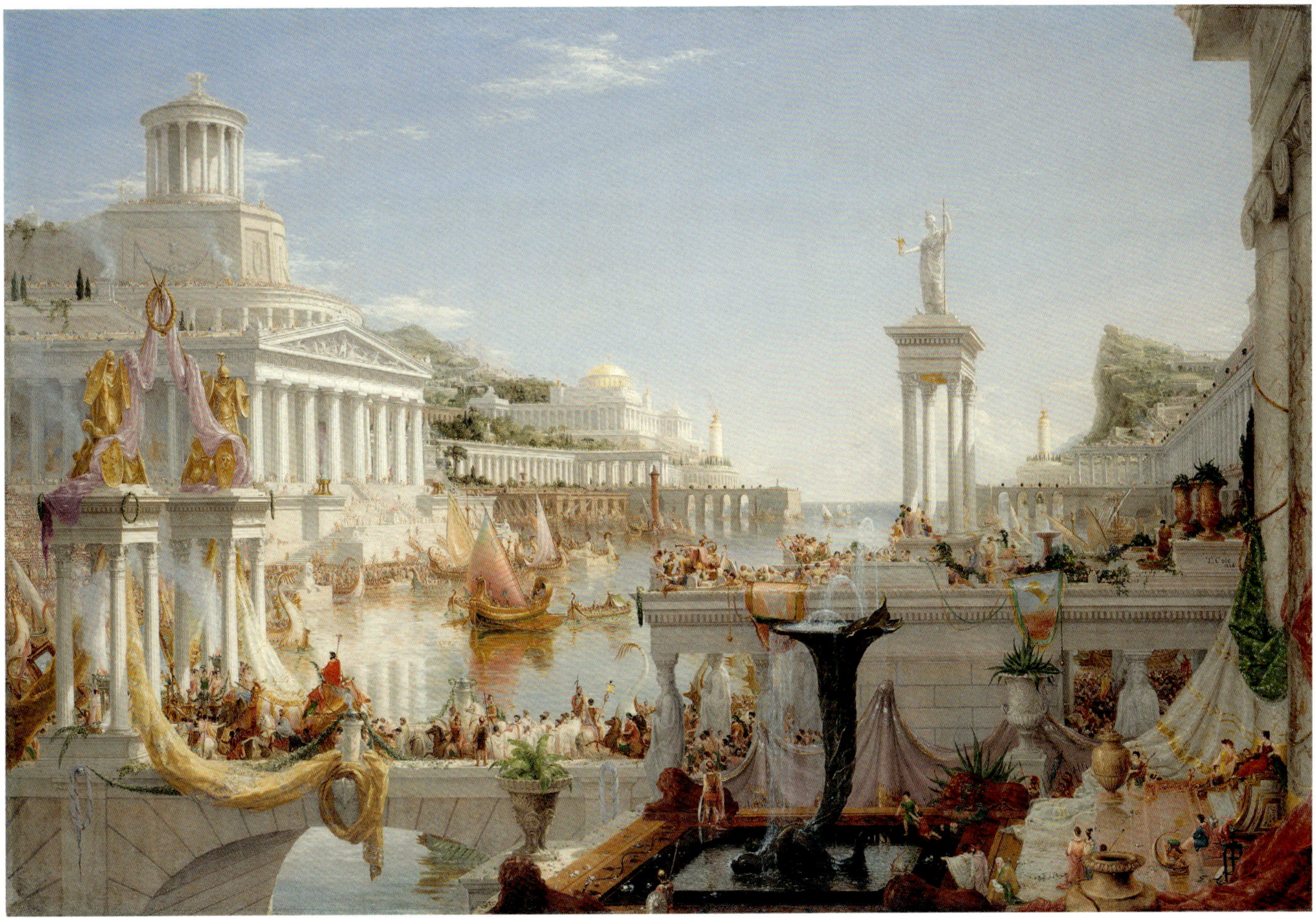

11 Thomas Cole (1801–1848), *The Course of Empire: The Consummation of Empire*, 1835–6, oil on canvas, 130.2 × 193 cm, New-York Historical Society. Gift of The New York Gallery of the Fine Arts (1858.3)

'splendid combinations of colour ... destitute of all appearance of solidity'.[25] He also visited Turner's private gallery in Queen Anne's Gate, where he admired *Dido building Carthage* and other historical landscapes. After returning to the United States, Cole embarked on *The Course of Empire* (1834–6), a series of five paintings, each denoting the condition or 'state' of an ancient civilisation – savage, arcadian, consummation, destruction and desolation – thus charting its rise and fall.[26] The centrepiece, *The Consummation of Empire* (fig. 11), drew on his experiences of Rome and the seaports of both Claude and Turner, though purposely removing all their subtlety and (in Turner's case) ambiguity, to create 'a vivid panorama of the vainglorious maturity of a powerful empire'.[27] This cautionary tale, critiquing unbridled imperialism and industrialisation, targeted his fellow Americans as well as Europeans. But in setting a new standard for historical landscape in the United States, Cole's paintings equally demonstrate how American artists embraced and reimagined European art. They are also emblematic of how Turner came to play an increasingly important role, before and after his death in 1851, in the artistic culture of North America, above all as the great moderniser of the old master tradition – which is precisely how Turner sought to promote himself. When Cole met him in December 1829, Turner had already drafted his first will, stipulating that two of his paintings, *Dido building Carthage* and *The Decline of the Carthaginian Empire*, should hang in perpetuity at the National Gallery with Claude's *Embarkation of the Queen of Sheba* (fig. 2) and *Landscape with the Marriage of Isaac and Rebekah ('The Mill')*.[28]

This significant intervention by Turner was first and foremost an attempt to secure a place in art history and the nation's cultural life, but on his own terms. It was also, perhaps, an acknowledgement by the artist that his determination to steer his own course would likely enthuse, divide and provoke critics and audiences still further. And so it proved to be. But the increasingly vociferous attacks Turner suffered, most famously in response to *Snow Storm – Steam-Boat off a Harbour's Mouth* (Tate, London) in 1842, resulted in another crucial intervention, this time by the young art critic John Ruskin (1819–1900). From the first volume of his *Modern Painters* (1843–60), Ruskin was to offer a comprehensive re-evaluation of Turner's later work, positioning him not only as the most important landscape painter in Western art, but as *the* artist who had liberated himself from the stifling conventions of past masters because he had remained true to the highest artistic principles with his uncompromising 'truth to nature'.[29] Ruskin later wrote that, in asserting Turner's 'perfect power', *Ulysses deriding Polyphemus* should be considered as 'the *central picture*' in his career, because the painting showed how the artist had moved from creating contrasts based on traditional chiaroscuro (light and dark) to ones based purely on colour, the technique Turner would use going forward.[30]

Ruskin would eventually own two oils by Turner, including *Slave Ship* of 1840, and around 30 watercolours. And his single-minded admiration for the artist encouraged a new audience from the 1840s for his paintings, many of which remained unsold. This was above all true in the United States, where Ruskin's published works were considered essential reading. In 1845, the genre painter C.R. Leslie (1794–1859), of American parentage and a frequent visitor to Turner's gallery, was engaged by the wealthy New York collector James Lenox (1800–1880) to acquire one of Turner's oil paintings. In an exchange with Turner (published in 1860), it seems that *The Fighting Temeraire* (fig. 16) was in Lenox's sights, but the artist had probably already decided to include that work in his bequest to the National Gallery. Ultimately, *Staffa, Fingal's Cave* (fig. 12) was chosen and thus became the first of his oils to cross the Atlantic.[31]

Only a few years before he died, in 1848, Turner amended his will to include all the finished pictures in his possession in the bequest to the Gallery. This would make him by far the most represented artist in the national collection. His prominence in the collection displays at the National Gallery (especially after 1876, when the whole bequest was reunited at Trafalgar Square) reinforced the growing perception among visitors, artists, collectors and connoisseurs alike that Turner was a central figure in the history of Western art. Consequently, in the United States, the momentum to acquire his works intensified during the late nineteenth century in private and public spheres, alongside other admired British artists such as Constable, Thomas Gainsborough (1727–1788) and Joshua Reynolds (1723–1792). By 1900, for example, the Metropolitan Museum of Art, New York, and the Museum of Fine Arts, Boston, owned Turner's *Whalers* (about 1845) and *Slave Ship* respectively. Among wealthy private collectors, the first 30 years of the next century saw the purchase of more than 20 major oil paintings. These included *Keelmen heaving in Coals by Moonlight* (fig. 5) and its companion *Venice: The Dogana and San Giorgio Maggiore* (1834), both bought by Peter Widener of Pennsylvania in 1910 and now in the National Gallery of Art, Washington, DC; and *Dieppe* and *Cologne*, purchased by Henry Clay Frick in 1914, adding to the Antwerp and Calais harbour scenes by Turner he already owned. The influence of the National Gallery on collectors like Frick cannot be overstated. In 1909, his daughter, Helen, described an afternoon visit to the Gallery with her mother, where they admired 'some wonderful Turners' among the many 'outstanding' old master paintings. She concluded, 'I could spend my entire life there.'[32]

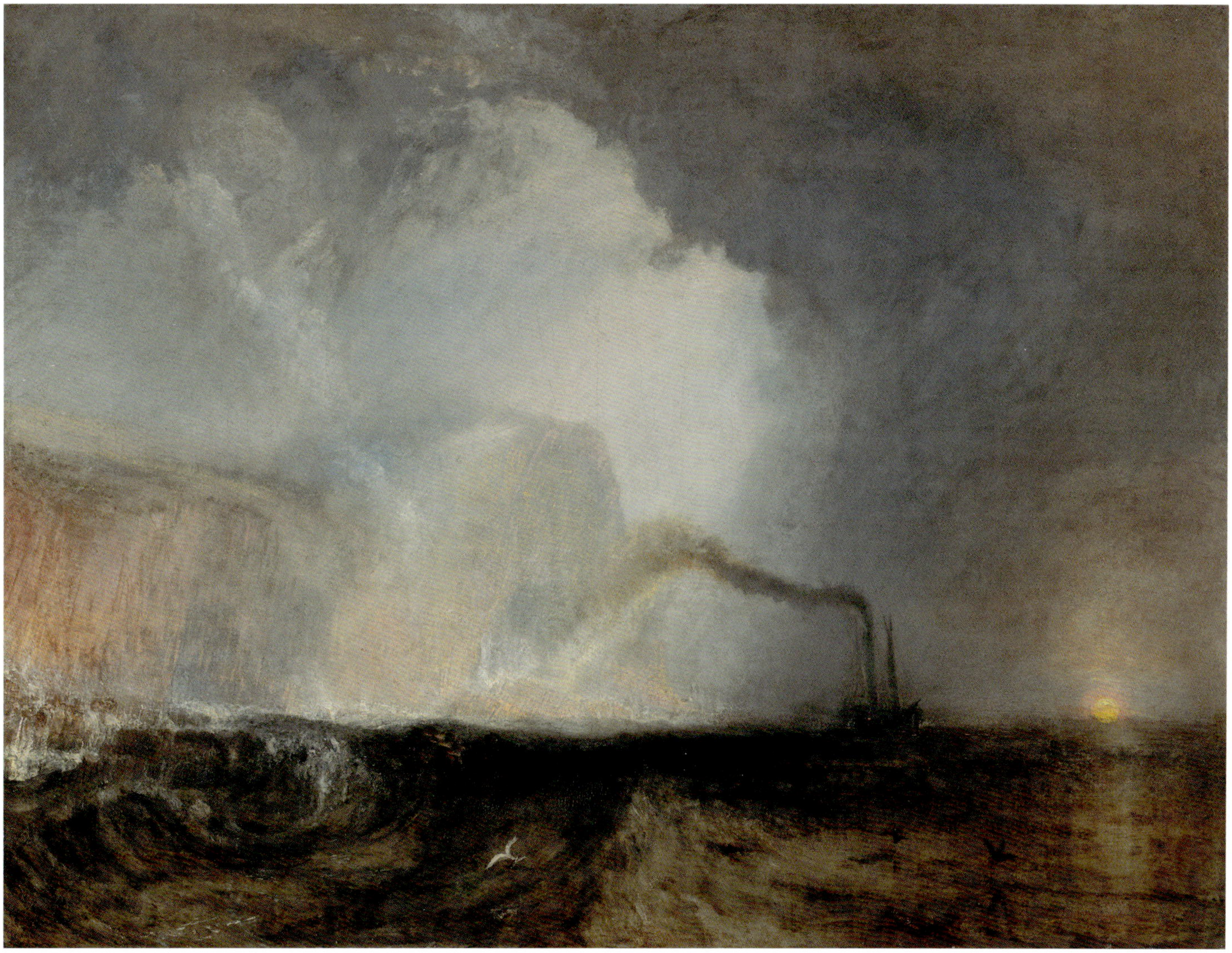

12 *Staffa, Fingal's Cave*, about 1831–2, oil on canvas, 90.8 × 121.3 cm, Yale Center for British Art, Paul Mellon Collection, New Haven, Connecticut (B1978.43.14)

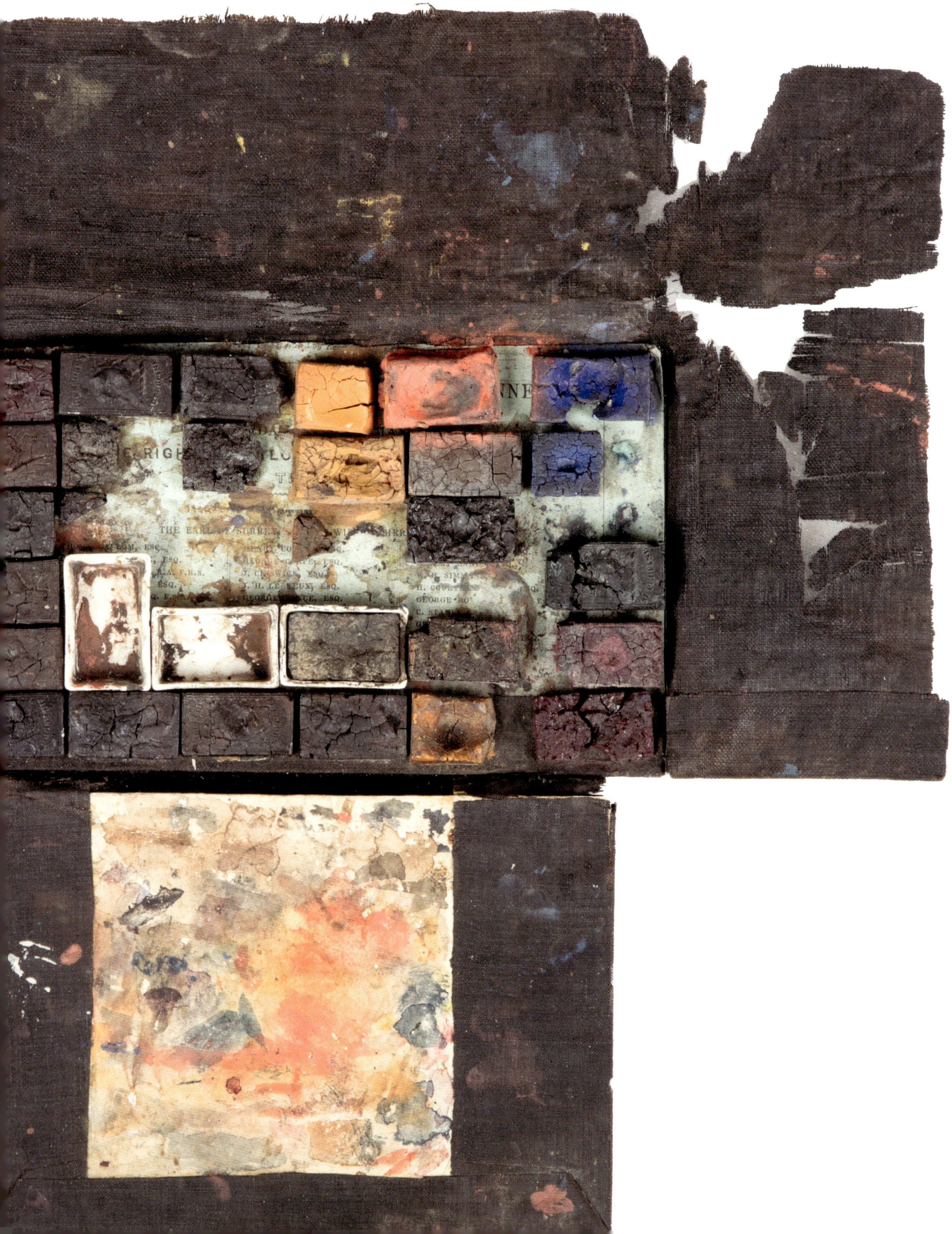

TURNER AS AN ARTIST-TRAVELLER

Thomas Ardill

From the age of 17 in 1792 until he reached 70 in 1845, J.M.W. Turner went travelling around the UK or the continent almost every summer. Like other landscape artists, he made the most of the long days and clement weather to collect raw material for his pictures before settling down in the autumn to start painting for the Royal Academy's annual exhibition in May. For much of the season he was on the move, touring from place to place, observing the landscape as he moved through it and making short stops to study sites of particular interest in more detail. Anything that had pictorial potential, or that added to his knowledge and understanding of landscape, nature, architecture, people or place, would be jotted down in a sketchbook and committed to memory.

After his death nearly 300 sketchbooks were found in Turner's studio, along with individual sheets – a total of approximately 37,000 pages of drawings and watercolours (figs 14, 15). As the artist frequently used a single page for multiple sketches, he must have made hundreds of thousands of drawings during his career, the vast majority of them while on tour. This provided him with a huge archive from which most of his oil paintings, watercolours and engraving designs were developed.[1] Of equal importance, though, were his memory – which was capable of fleshing out the details, colours and atmosphere of places he had often only recorded in the most cursory way – and his imagination, which was fired by the places he visited.[2]

Turner was notoriously private and relayed very few of his experiences of travel to friends and colleagues, except to complain about difficult conditions or recall a minor misadventure. Early reports of those who encountered him on sketching tours suggest

13 Travelling watercolour box owned by J.M.W. Turner, about 1842, 29.6 × 31.7 × 0.9 cm, Royal Academy of Arts, London (03/7072)

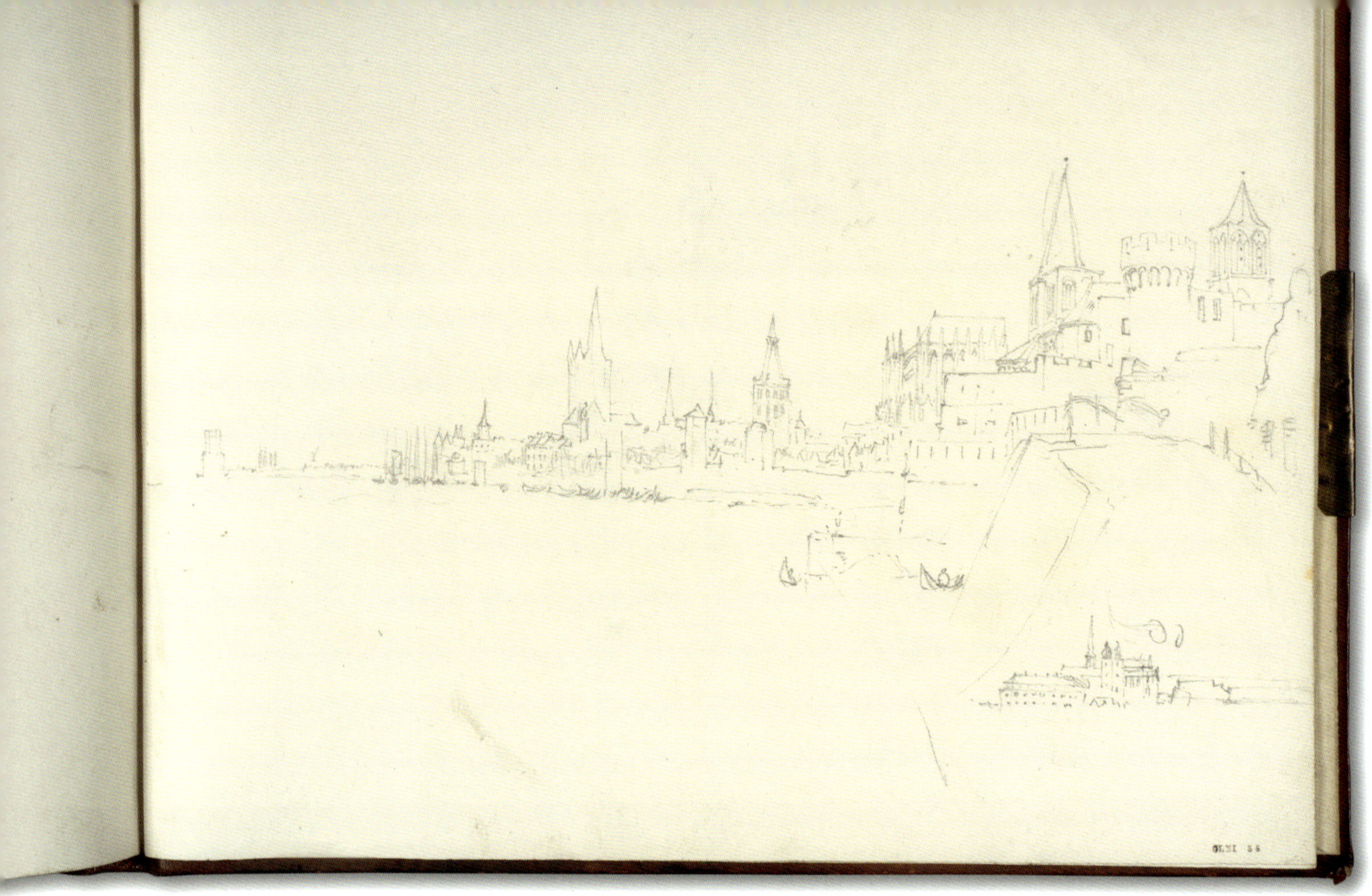

14 *River Front at Cologne, looking Upstream with the Bayenturm, Groß St Martin's, Town Hall, Choir of Cathedral and St Cunibert's: Deutz on East Bank of the Rhine*, 1817, *Rhine* sketchbook, graphite on paper, 20.2 × 26.5 cm, Tate, London (D12985; CLXI 55)

that his seriousness and single-mindedness were often to the fore. The Narraways, family friends with whom he spent his first sketching tour in Bristol in 1791, described him as 'not like young people in general, he was singular and very silent, seemed exclusively devoted to his drawing, would not go into society', although 'People could not help but like him because he was so good humoured.'[3] Many who met him seem not to have known quite what to make of this jocular but hard-working, somewhat mysterious artist. Nearly 40 years later, an Italian merchant travelling by coach to Bologna observed a very similar, though older, man:

> a good-tempered, funny, little, elderly gentleman ... He is continually popping his head out of [the] window to sketch whatever strikes his fancy, and became quite angry because the conductor would not wait for him whilst he took a sunrise view of Macerara ... From his conversation he is evidently near kin to, if not absolutely, an artist. Probably you know something of him. The name on his trunk is, J.W. or J.M.W. Turner![4]

Turner rarely advertised his profession while travelling, even if he could not entirely disguise it with a pencil and sketchbook in hand. When he checked into a hotel in Cherbourg during a tour of the Loire Valley in France in 1826, he gave his occupation as 'Rentier' (a man of independent financial means) and the purpose of his visit as 'pour de [sic] promener' (for walking).[5] Similarly, in Guernsey, five years later, he is listed in the steamboat passengers' log as a 'Gentleman' rather than an artist.[6] He was even more private when it came to his working practices, frequently refusing to allow people to see his sketches.[7] In 1818, he even pursued the Reverend

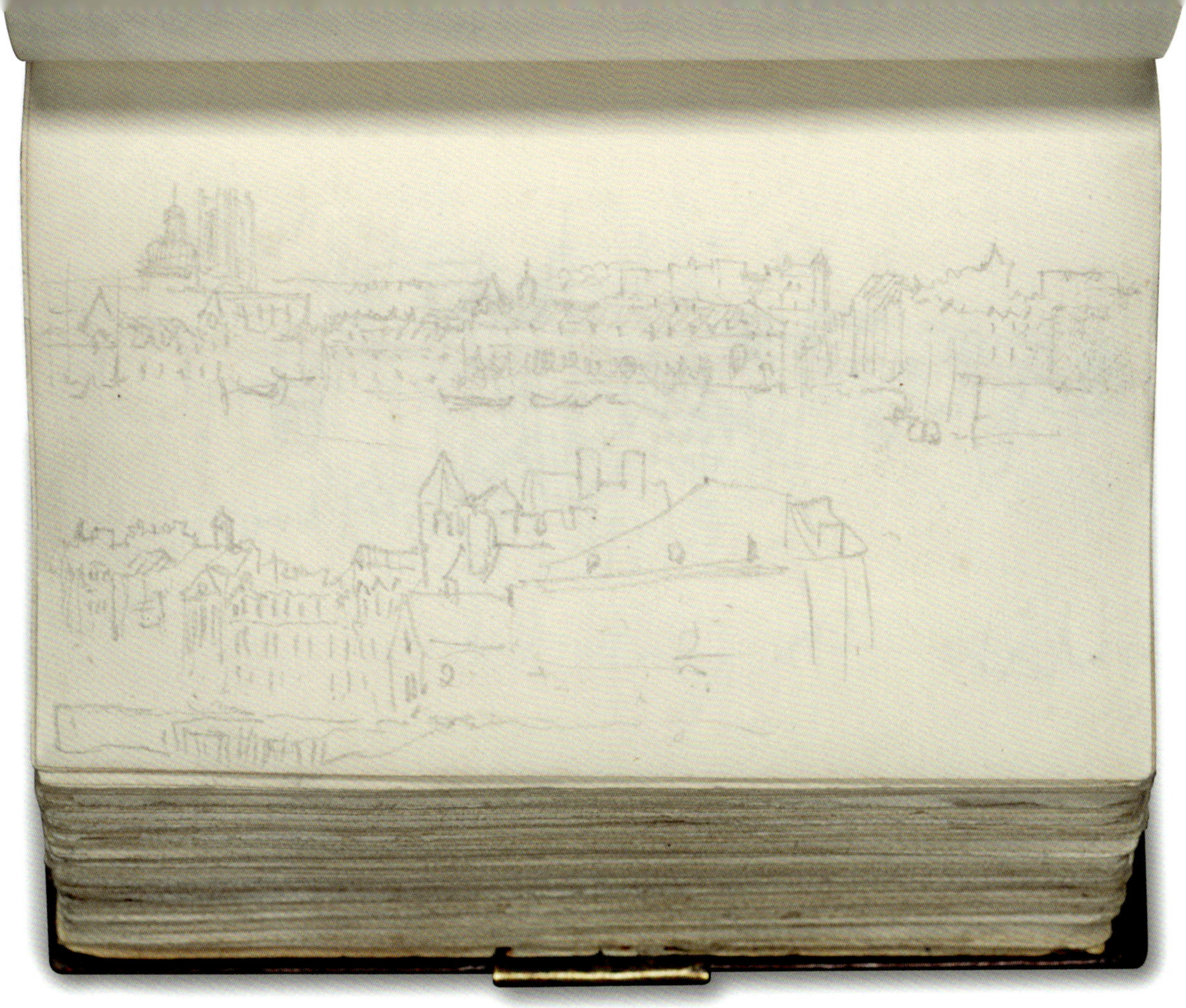

15 *Dieppe*, 1824, *Rivers Meuse and Moselle* sketchbook, graphite on paper, 7.8 × 11.8 cm, Tate, London (D20005; CCXVI 231a)

John Thomson's wife around the room when she tried to look at his day's work: 'Turner saw it and gave chase, caught her, and took the book from her before she had time to even open it.'[8] Such (frequently humorous) anecdotes, along with the evidence of Turner's work and working practices that we shall turn to shortly, offer glimpses into his identity as an artist-traveller. As we shall see, it was an identity that shifted throughout his career. Based on a mixture of selective memory, mediated and partially fictionalised commentary, and pure fantasy, our picture of Turner on tour remains elusive.

ARTISTS ON TOUR

Turner's 50 years as a travelling artist coincided with a number of changes in the art market, international relations and technology that profoundly influenced his career and artistic identity. He witnessed the decline of the traditional Grand Tour and took part in the birth of modern middle-class tourism; indeed, his works did much to fuel public desire to travel. This period also coincided with new opportunities in the print market and a boom in topographical publications (see Christine Riding's essay in this volume, p. 13).

The concept of the Grand Tour originated with an influential guidebook, *The Voyage of Italy* (1670), in which travel writer Richard Lassels (about 1603–1668) laid out the benefits to young noblemen of completing their education with a visit to France and Italy in preparation for a life of public duty.[9] Their principal activities, he proposed, should be to see the places associated with classical history and culture, experience the world, and collect paintings, sculptures, books and souvenirs. During the eighteenth century,

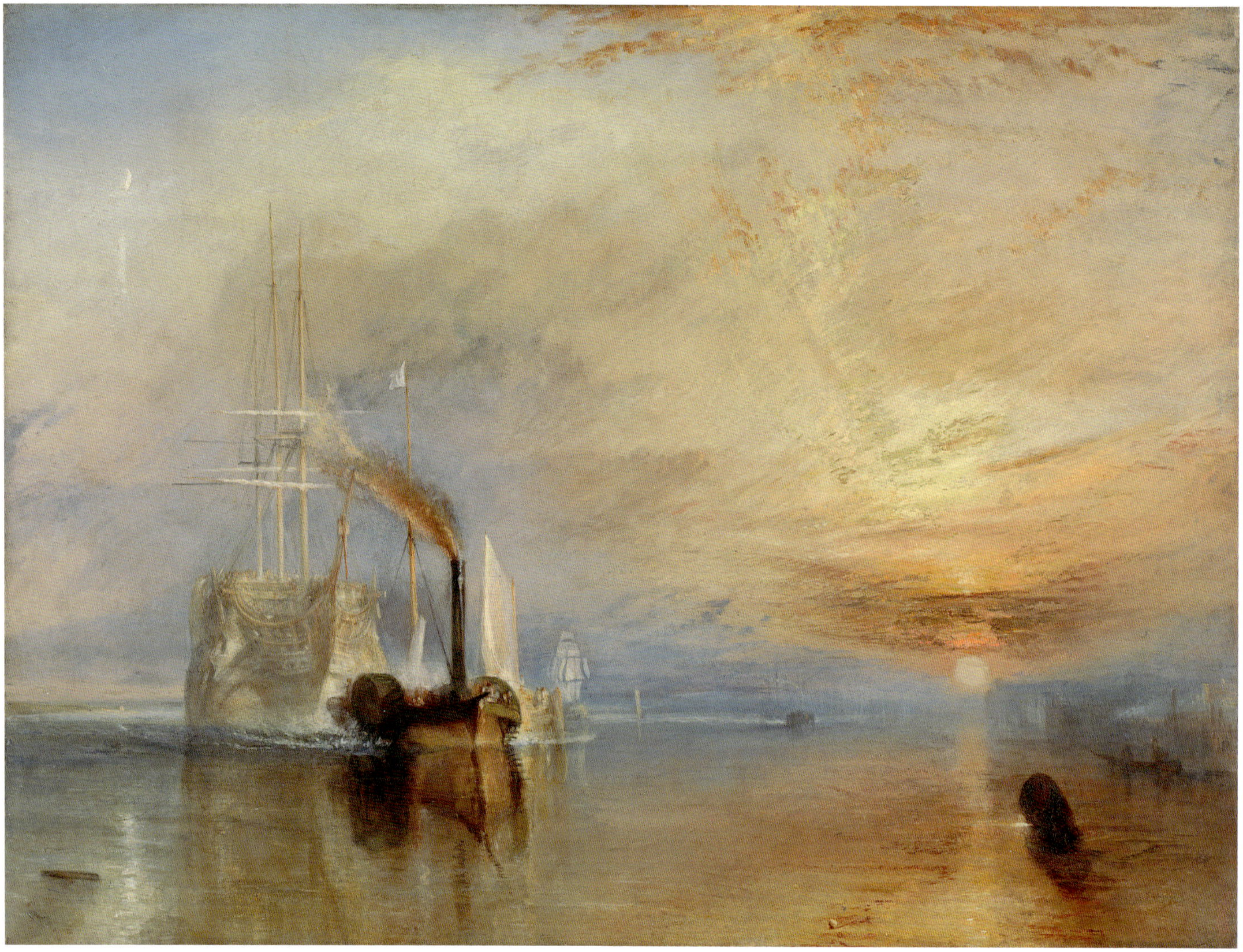

16 *The Fighting Temeraire tugged to her last berth to be broken up, 1838*, 1839, oil on canvas, 90.7 × 121.6 cm, The National Gallery, London (NG524)

the number of British Grand Tourists swelled: the nobility and gentry were joined by the sons and eventually the daughters of the wealthy, as well as the arts professionals who supported their education and helped them to assemble private collections. Artists were financed by the wealthier class of Grand Tourist through sponsorship, commissions, art sales and fees for tutoring, working as agents or dealers. Many early Royal Academicians – including some of those who taught or influenced Turner, such as Joshua Reynolds, Richard Wilson (1713/14–1782) and Benjamin West (1738–1820) – benefited from a Grand Tour sponsored by aristocratic patrons, or worked in Rome for the tourist market. This enabled them to study the works of the old masters and bring their practice in line with the revered examples of Claude (fig. 2), Nicolas Poussin (1594–1665) and other painters whose works were being eagerly amassed by the English aristocracy. If Turner had been a little older he might have joined them, but his entry into the Royal Academy Schools in 1789 coincided with the beginning of the French Revolution, and in 1796, the year he exhibited his first oil painting at the Academy,[10] Napoleon occupied Italy and travel in Europe became impossible. Nevertheless, Turner made the most

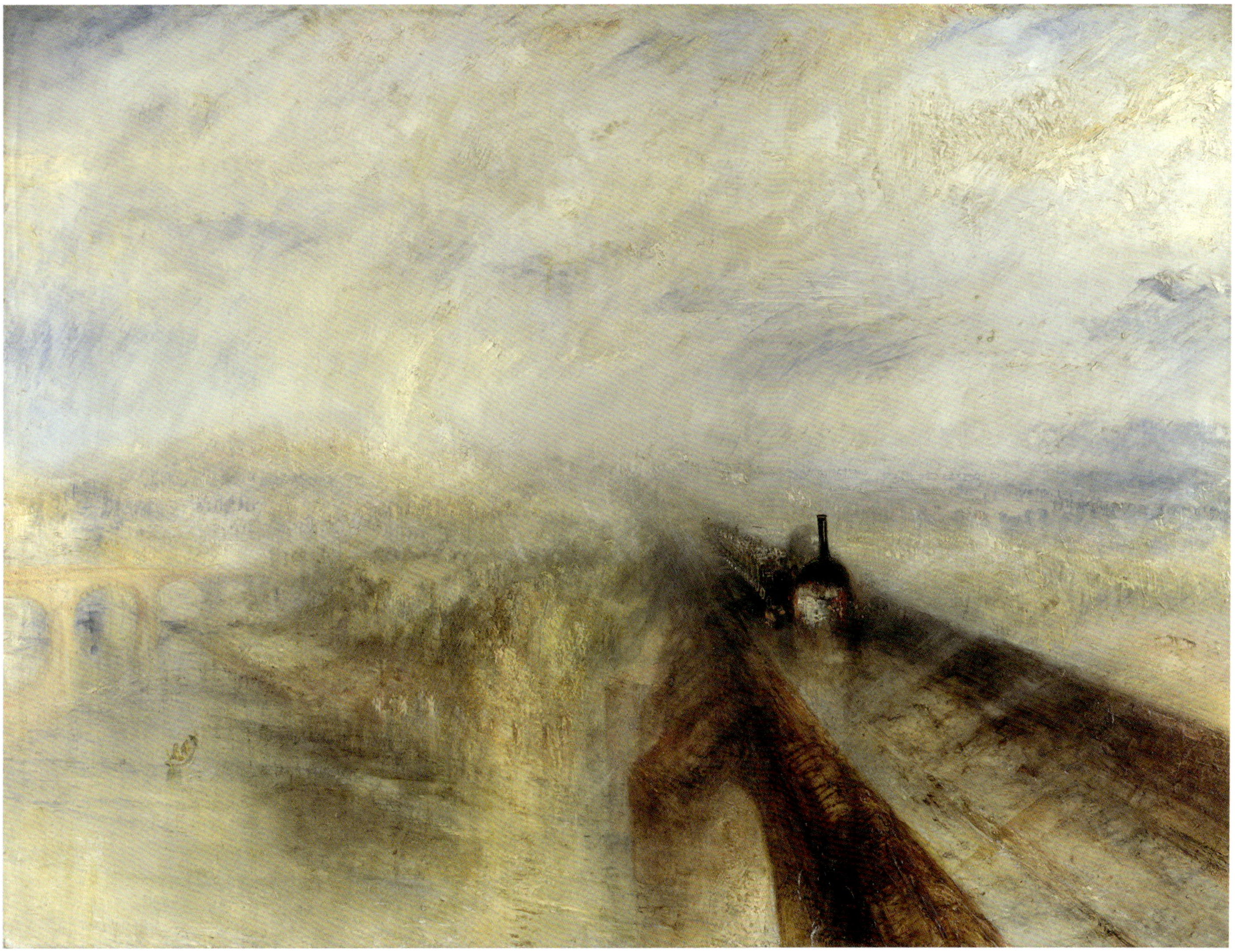

17 *Rain, Steam and Speed – The Great Western Railway*, 1844, oil on canvas, 91 × 121.8 cm, The National Gallery, London (NG538)

of the English, Welsh and Scottish landscapes that were already popular tourist destinations and would figure largely in his oeuvre when he began visiting them on sketching tours. A 1791 visit to friends at Bristol marked his first such tour, resulting in the *Bristol and Malmesbury* sketchbook (VI, Tate, London).[11]

Many British artists, including Turner, Maria Cosway (1760–1838), Joseph Farington (1747–1821) and John Opie (1761–1807), took advantage of a brief respite in the European conflict in 1802–3 by travelling to France or Switzerland, but it was not until the end of the Napoleonic Wars in 1815 that regular travel on the continent was made possible. This ushered in the beginning of a new age of tourism that benefited not only from a long period of relative peace in Europe, but also from infrastructural and technological improvements that made travel much easier, quicker and more affordable. Artists like Turner along with poets like Lord Byron (1788–1824), Walter Scott (1771–1832) and Samuel Rogers (1763–1855), as well as middle-class tourists who flocked to see Restoration France and the battlefield of Waterloo, found that there had been significant improvements to roads and coach services under Napoleon.[12] It has been estimated, for example, that in 1818 alone some 2,000 British people visited Rome, the prime destination of the European Grand Tour, which Turner would visit for the first time the following year.

The growing number of guidebooks published in the 1820s and 1830s, regularly updated with information about new routes and improved accommodation affordable to the middle classes, reflects the growth in international tourism.[13] As shall be shown, Turner made use of these, and even contributed to the popularity of travel literature. Tourists and travellers of other kinds appear frequently in both his sketches and his finished work, like the ferry boat crowded with female tourists at the centre of *Cologne, the Arrival of a Packet-Boat: Evening* (cat. 2). Within a few years, steamboats made travel along Europe's rivers and coasts much faster, enabling Turner to cover more distance over the summer months and fuelling his interest in river scenery.[14] Railways followed in the 1830s, although he made limited use of them. The National Gallery's most celebrated paintings by Turner, *The Fighting Temeraire tugged to her last berth to be broken up, 1838* (fig. 16) and *Rain, Steam, and Speed – The Great Western Railway* (fig. 17), exhibited in 1839 and 1844 respectively, are both complex and innovative reflections on the impact of the Industrial Revolution on the age of travel.

Another technology that profoundly affected Turner's career as a touring artist was the invention of steel engraving and its adoption as a means of artistic reproduction in England in 1820. Steel plates had an advantage over the traditional copper in that they were much harder, and able to withstand thousands rather than hundreds of impressions. As a result, prints became more affordable and reached a much wider audience, creating new commercial opportunities for landscape artists. Between 1811 and 1839 Turner enjoyed continuous employment, first working on a series of topographical part-works such as *Picturesque Views in England and Wales* (1827–38), and later on illustrated volumes of poetry by Scott, Byron, Rogers and Thomas Campbell (1777–1844) (see Christine Riding's essay in this volume, p. 13). These commissions from commercial publishers funded his trips and liberated him from financial reliance on private patrons (although, as will be seen, he did sometimes receive funding from them too). Such ambitious projects also fed into his artistic identity. One of these series, dedicated to views along French rivers and issued in three volumes between 1833 and 1835, was *Turner's Annual Tour*: a title that firmly established his reputation as a travelling artist and provided a commentary that shaped his identity.

'SEARCHING AFTER EFFECTS': WHY TURNER TRAVELLED

Turner's annual summer journeys were central to his training and development as an artist, the range of his subject matter, his commercial success, and his own lifestyle and sense of self. Some of his trips were primarily intended as holidays, including regular visits to Walter Fawkes (1769–1825) at Farnley Hall in North Yorkshire, the 3rd Earl of Egremont, George Wyndham (1751–1837) at Petworth, Sussex, and John Nash (1752–1835) on the Isle of Wight. These were occasions for relaxation and socialising, but they also helped Turner to cement his relationships with colleagues and patrons and afforded him the space and encouragement to experiment with subjects and techniques. Other journeys were geared towards work, in the form of study and practice, research and the gathering of raw material.

During his twenties, Turner followed the fashion for picturesque travel, seeking out landscapes that exemplified the aesthetic theories of the sublime and the picturesque and seeing the natural world through the lens of art. Initially limited to travelling within the British Isles, he made several journeys to Wales and Scotland during the 1790s, exploring appropriate landscapes and 'searching after effects', which the theorist Reverend William

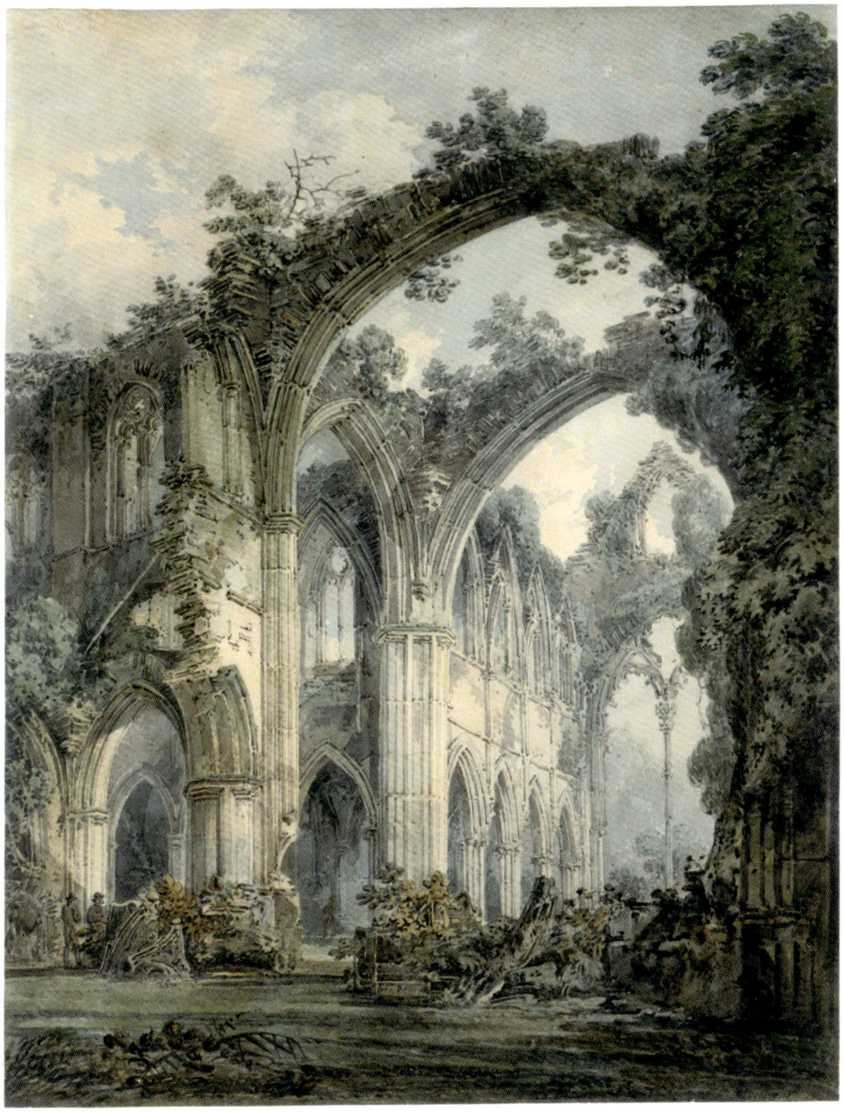

18 *Interior of Tintern Abbey, Monmouthshire*, about 1794, watercolour and graphite pencil on paper, 42 × 58.4 cm, Victoria and Albert Museum, London (1683-1871)

Gilpin (1724–1804) had defined as 'the general intention of picturesque travel'.[15] Tintern Abbey in Monmouthshire was a particularly popular destination at this time, thanks to its description in Gilpin's *Observations on the River Wye* (1782), and Turner visited in 1792 and again the following year to study the famous ruins, later working his sketches up into watercolours (fig. 18). Several versions of the view of the interior even include tourists who gaze up at the decaying arches, inviting the viewer to follow them and the artist in a studied appreciation of the architecture and its setting.[16]

The success of Turner's exhibition watercolours, and the oil paintings that followed from 1796, secured his election as an associate member of the Royal Academy before the end of the decade. This was followed by full membership in 1802, opening new doors for the artist. Three collectors clubbed together that year to fund his first trip to the continent, so that he could study the paintings recently installed in the Museé Central des Arts at the Louvre and see something of French and Swiss landscapes. Charles Anderson-Pelham, 1st Earl of Yarborough (1781–1846), who organised the trip and was the referee for Turner's first passport, would certainly have expected his investment to yield results; he was presumably satisfied when Turner exhibited *The Festival of the Opening of the Vintage at Mâcon* (Sheffield City Art Galleries) at the Royal Academy in 1803, as he purchased it the following year for 300 guineas.[17] This work, with its celebratory subject, was a double justification for the expenditure of Turner's patrons as he combined in it a French landscape scene with the artistic influence of the old masters he had studied in Paris, especially the works of Claude (see Christine Riding's essay in this volume, p. 12).[18] With its Arcadian subject matter, the work demonstrated a classical artistic sensibility, reflecting Turner's credentials as a graduate of the Grand Tour.

But Turner was also seeking the very antithesis of such landscapes in 1802. His painting of *Calais Pier* (fig. 19), also included in the 1803 exhibition, took its inspiration from the Dutch tradition of marine painting, while its subject matter – a near miss between a fishing vessel and a crowded packet boat – brings us closer to the category of the sublime. It was apparently inspired by personal experience, as Turner's 'landing at Calais [was] nearly swampt', according to a note in his sketchbook.[19] Mâcon was simply a stop on the way to Geneva and the Swiss Alps, where he sought out the dramatic landscapes associated with the sublime.[20] On his return Turner was pleased to report to Joseph Farington that he had found the 'fragments

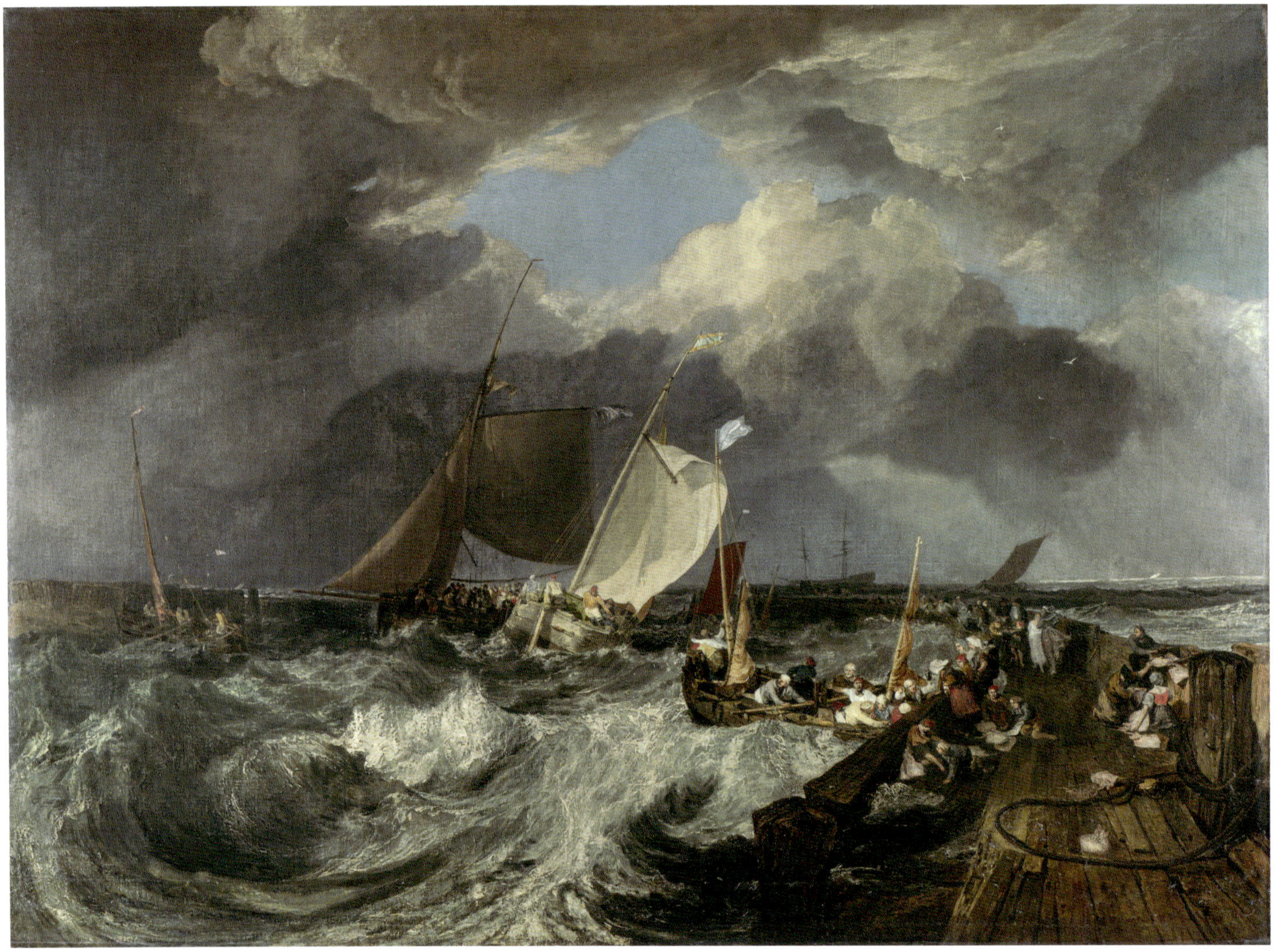

19 *Calais Pier, with French Poissards preparing for Sea: an English Packet arriving*, 1803, oil on canvas, 172 × 240 cm, The National Gallery, London (NG472)

and precipices very romantic, and strikingly grand. The country on the whole surpasses Wales; and Scotland too.'[21] The 'fragments and precipices' that Turner traversed in order to see and paint sublime scenery played an important part in constructing an image of the artist as an adventurer. In his 1831 watercolour, *Loch Coruisk, Skye* (fig. 20), we see two tiny figures perched precariously on a narrow summit; they appear to be sketching. The detail recalls the now iconic image of the Romantic traveller by Turner's contemporary Caspar David Friedrich (1774–1840), *The Wanderer above the Sea of Fog* (fig. 21) – a coincidence, as that painting was not known in the UK until the twentieth century. Just as the Wanderer is often interpreted as being Friedrich himself, we know (thanks to a note in the illustrated edition of Walter Scott's *Poetical Works*, for which *Loch Coruisk* was engraved) that one of Turner's mountaineers is intended as a self-portrait. Scott's editor recounts a story about the artist's treacherous climb, claiming that 'but for one or two tufts of grass he must have broken his neck, having slipped when trying to attain the best position for taking the view'.[22]

Turner produced several works inspired by the unpredictable experiences of travel.[23] In 1829 he memorialised a particularly bad return journey from Italy, during which the

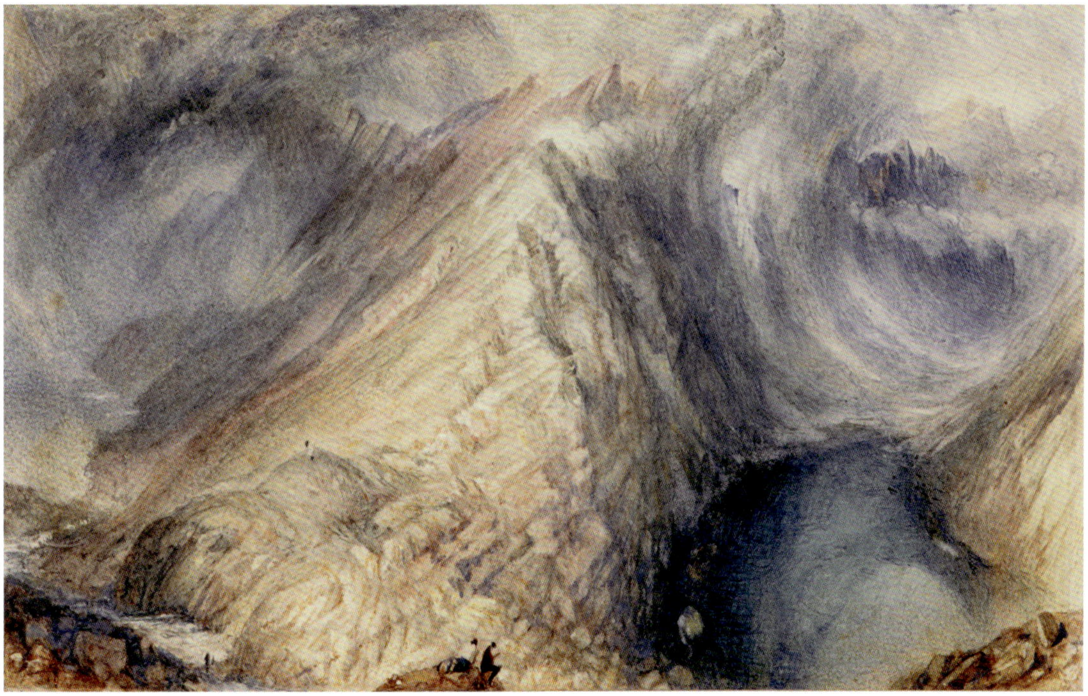

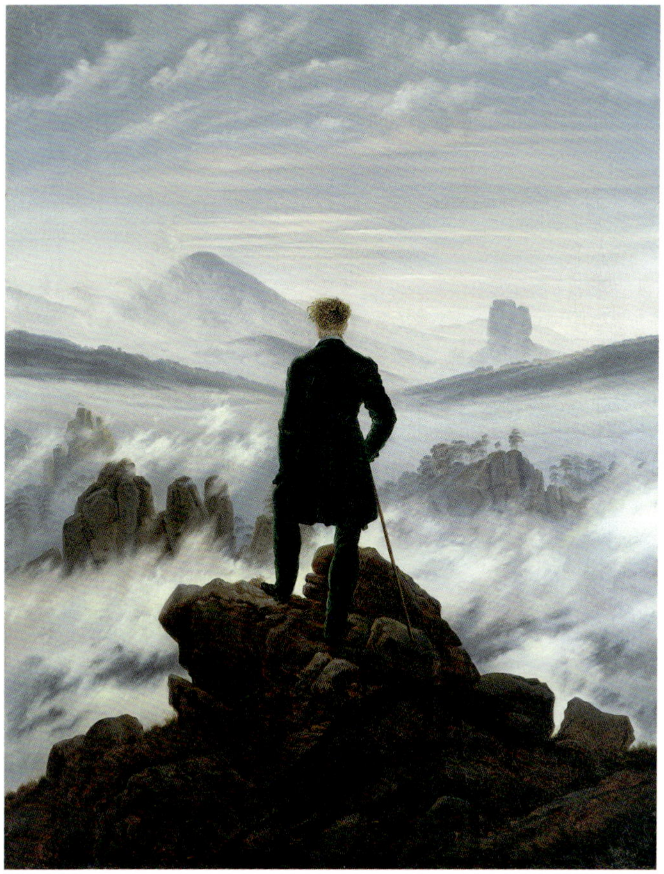

20 *Loch Coruisk, Skye*, 1831, watercolour with scraping on paper, 8.9 × 14.3 cm, Scottish National Gallery (D NG 861)

21 Caspar David Friedrich (1774–1840), *The Wanderer above the Sea of Fog*, about 1817, oil on canvas, 94.8 × 74.8 cm, Hamburger Kunsthalle, Hamburg (HK-5161)

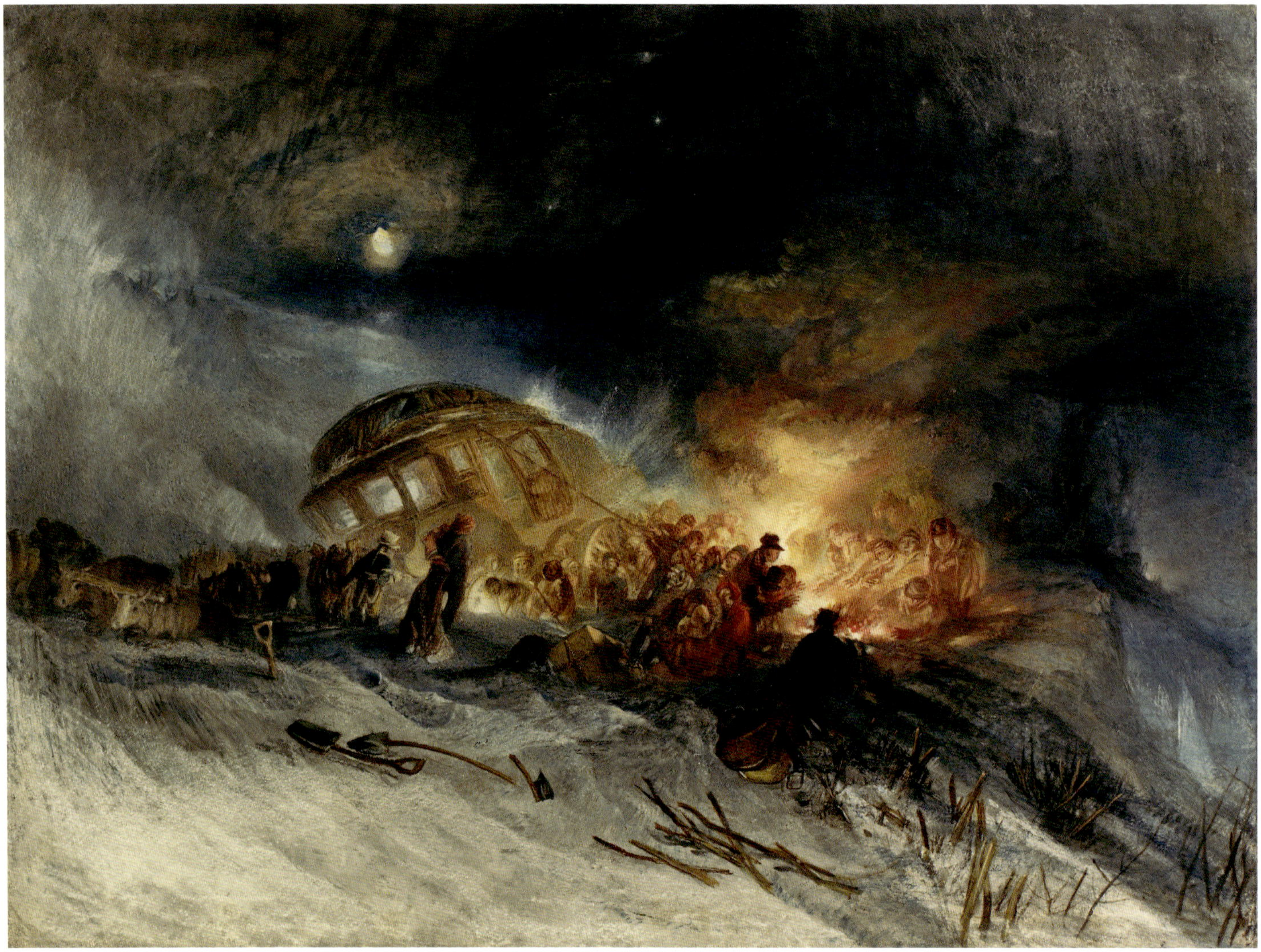

22 *Messieurs les Voyageurs on their Return from Italy (par la diligence) in a Snow Drift upon Mount Tarrar – 22nd of January, 1829*, 1829, watercolour on paper, 54.5 × 74.7 cm, The British Museum, London (1958,0712.431)

coach he was travelling in 'zizd [sic] into a ditch and required 6 oxen, sent three miles back for, to drag it out'. The artist, who may be depicted top-hatted and huddling by the fire in a grand exhibition watercolour he made of the memory (fig. 22), recalled in a letter how he 'bivouacked in the snow with fires lighted for 3 Hours on Mont Tarate [sic] while the diligence [public coach] was righted and dug out'.[24] This and similar incidents recalled by Turner are reminders that travel, especially in the remoter parts of Europe and in poor weather, was still a risky activity in the early nineteenth century.[25] Turner was certainly willing to risk these dangers and evidently took some pride in having experienced them, suggesting that a sense of adventure (or misadventure) – almost obligatory for those who considered themselves to be travellers rather than tourists during this period – was one of the qualities that led him to consider himself a Romantic artist.[26]

The opportunity for sexual adventure may have been another attraction of travel for a committed bachelor like Turner. Several of his sketchbooks contain erotic drawings that suggest he, like many young male Grand Tourists, visited brothels while abroad – a supposition reinforced by the list of ingredients

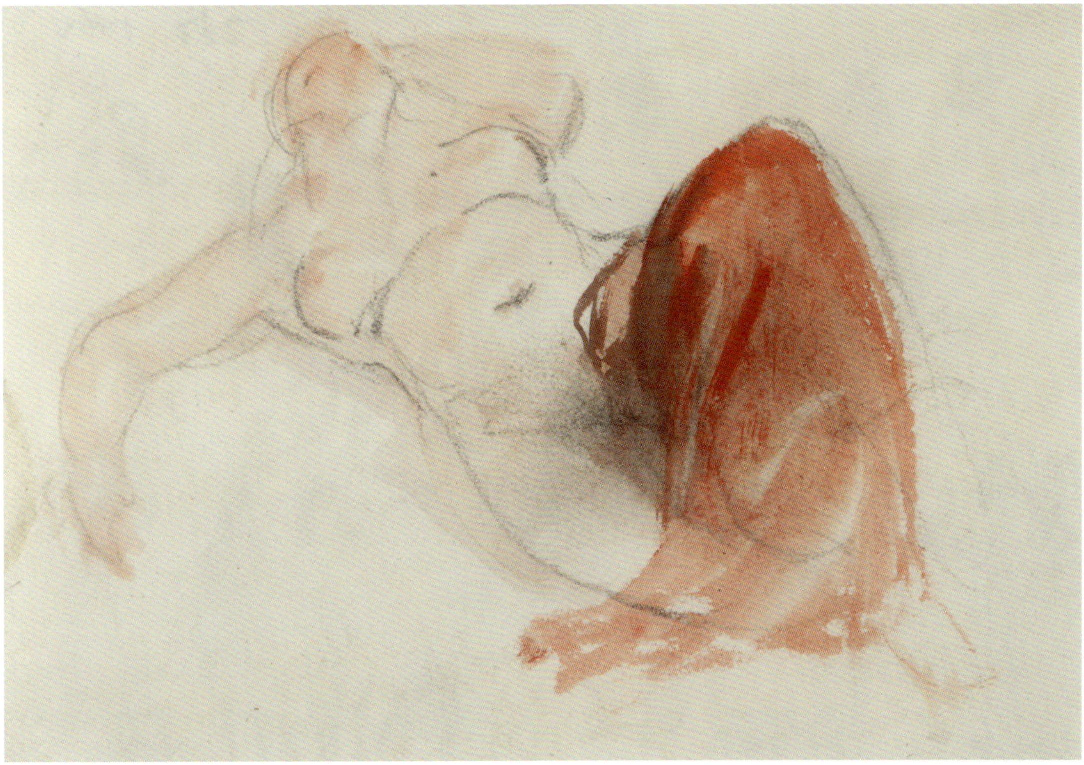

23 *Reclining Nude, draped with a Red Cloth*, 1821, *Paris, Seine and Dieppe* sketchbook, pencil and red watercolour on white wove paper, 11.3 × 18.9 cm, Tate, London (D18568; CCXI 28 a)

for a cure for gonorrhoea noted in one of his sketchbooks.[27] The 1821 *Paris, Seine and Dieppe* sketchbook includes, among its views of Dieppe harbour and French figure studies, a wash drawing of a naked woman loosely covered with red drapery and reclining on a bed or couch (fig. 23). Many of Turner's surviving erotic drawings were produced during his 1833 and 1840 tours of Venice, a city then associated with sexual licence. One watercolour, of two apparently half-naked women at a window conversing with men below, could well depict a Venetian brothel scene, though several scholars have attempted a Shakespearean interpretation.[28] Without written evidence, these hints are far from conclusive proof that the artist participated in sex tourism. But the scattering of erotic imagery found throughout his travel sketchbooks certainly points to the sensual appeal of passing through exciting foreign cities.

A variety of professional and personal motivations therefore played a role in Turner's itinerancy. But the primary purpose of most of his annual tours was to collect views for published series of topographical engravings. The income from these was his bread and butter from the 1810s to the 1830s, during which time he was continually contracted on an overlapping series of projects that funded many of his trips. Other journeys were made without existing commissions, but in the expectation that the resulting sketches might be used in the future. Turner's willingness to travel far, fast and frequently, combined with his elevation of topographical work far beyond prosaic view-taking, made him one of the most prolific landscape illustrators of the period. To keep up with demand, he had to plan his itineraries carefully and develop methods of working that were effective and efficient.

'TURNER'S FAVOURITE MODE OF PACKING': HOW HE TRAVELLED

With a few exceptions, Turner preferred to travel alone.[29] He made sure he was well prepared by researching locations, booking travel arrangements, planning routes and hotels and packing appropriately.

Turner usually had some idea in advance of the subjects he hoped to see, and therefore sought advice and consulted published resources before travelling. On two occasions he had guidebooks rebound with interleaved blank pages so that he could also use them for sketching.[30] In preparation for an 1819 trip to Italy he consulted the artist James Hakewill (1778–1843), with whom he was collaborating on a topographical publication called *A Picturesque Tour of Italy*.[31] Hakewill, who had visited the country in 1816–17, filled a pocket-sized notebook with written advice for Turner, including information on accommodation and sightseeing and a suggested itinerary of artworks, churches and museums to visit.[32] In another sketchbook Turner transcribed notes from J.C. Eustace's *Tour through Italy* (3rd edition, 1817) and copied thumbnail sketches from *Select Views in Italy* (1792–6) by John 'Warwick' Smith (1749–1831), William Byrne (1743–1805) and John Emes (1762–1810).

He prepared with similar care for a journey along the rivers Meuse, Moselle and Rhine in 1824, taken in connection with his proposed *Rivers of Europe* series and to make sketches at Dieppe.[33] In his *Rivers Meuse and Moselle* sketchbook, he drew maps and lists of towns and prepared a full timetable.[34] This plotted a course across the English Channel to Calais and via Brussels to Liège, where he would begin a journey down the Meuse as far as Verdun before heading east to Metz and up the Moselle to Koblenz (fig. 24). There he joined the Middle Rhine to Cologne and made his way back via Liège to Brussels, to return to Calais via Ostend. From Calais he took a detour to Dieppe, arriving

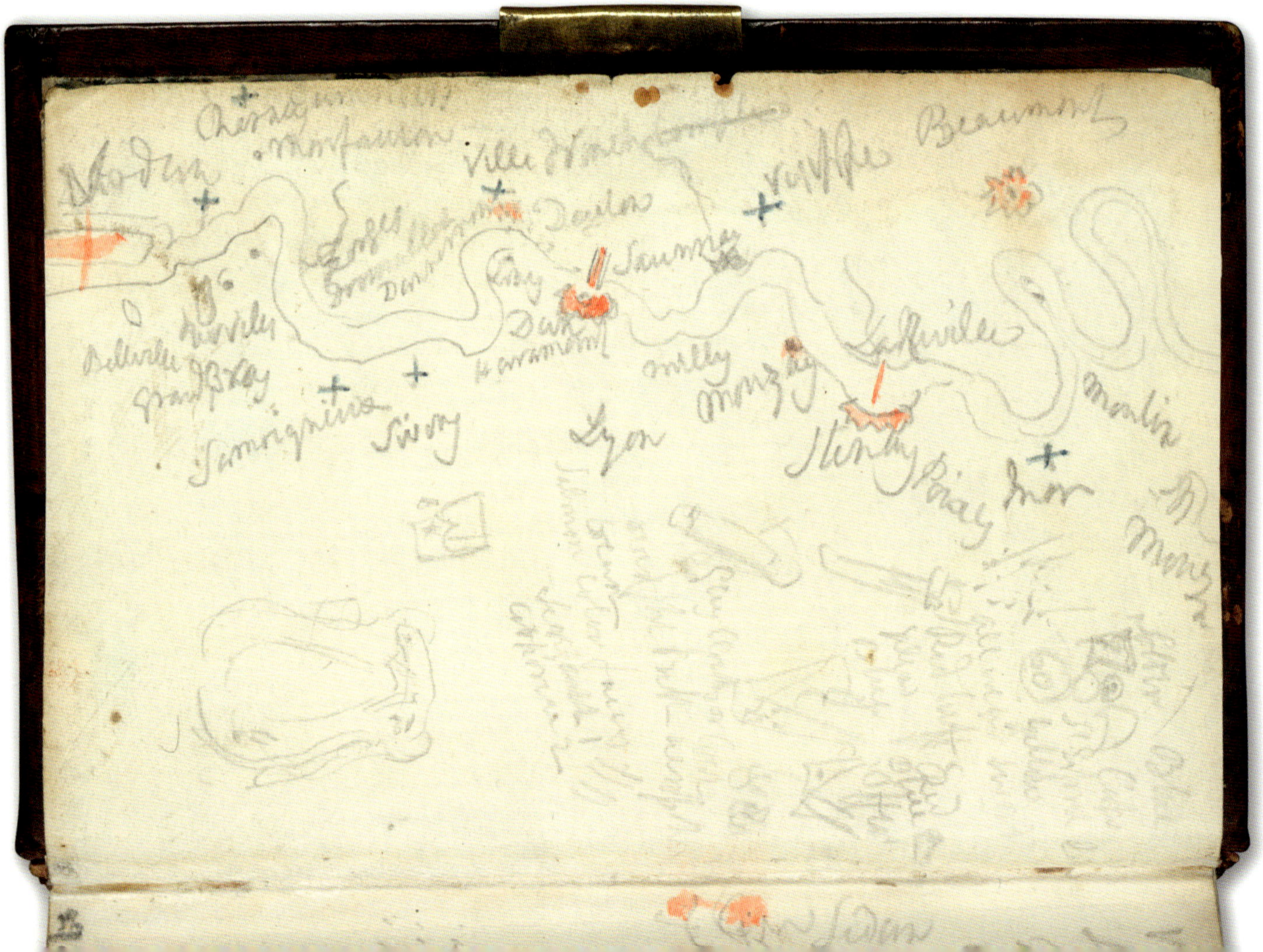

24 *Sketch Map of the Meuse between Verdun and Mouzon; Other Notes and Sketches*, 1824, *Rivers Meuse and Moselle* sketchbook, pencil and pen and red and blue ink on white wove paper, 7.8 × 11.8 cm, Tate, London (D40727; CCXVI)

on Friday, 11 September and staying a night before looping back to Calais and then home. Like many British tourists, he arranged all this with the assistance of Alois Wilhelm Schreiber's *Travellers' Guide down the Rhine* (1818). But when he came to preparing an 1826 trip to Brittany – an area of France not yet explored by British artists – there were no existing guidebooks in English, so Turner had to plan his route using a map purchased in France.[35] This journey off the beaten track was apparently taken without a prior commission, and so demonstrates his pioneering spirit as a traveller. It also points towards his entrepreneurship, as he eventually found a commercial outlet for the views he collected, teaming up with the publisher Charles Heath for the *Turner's Annual Tour* project.

A rare glimpse into how Turner packed for travel is offered by a list of clothes inscribed in his *Dolbadarn* sketchbook (1799–1800; XLVI, Tate, London), used on a tour of north-west England in 1799.[36] It represents a full trunk of clothes for the practicalities of travel (four under-waistcoats, six pairs cotton stockings, three boots, one greatcoat, one overall) as well as more formal attire (two pairs black silk stockings, eight cravats, four coloured waistcoats, one pair white silk stockings). Such heavy luggage may have been necessary for a journey broken by visits to the homes of wealthy patrons, but for trips requiring regular changes between diligences and steamboats and exploration on foot, Turner must have travelled much more lightly. This explains his practice of copying out relevant passages from guidebooks rather than carrying heavy volumes around with him. On some trips he apparently also took the precaution of packing a weapon, in the form of an umbrella with a concealed dagger in its handle, which he supposedly 'carried with him upon his Swiss and Italian journeys as a defence against brigands'.[37] Of course, his most prized possessions while on tour were his sketchbooks, of which he brought 23 to Italy in 1819 along with loose paper sheets, pencils and watercolours.[38]

'MAKING ROUGH PENCIL SKETCHES': HOW TURNER WORKED

Turner used a number of techniques to record the places he visited, but his primary method – the staple throughout his travels – was pencil on paper, often bound into sketchbooks. He used a variety of books, papers and drawing techniques throughout his career[39] but invariably carried at least one small notebook that could be stowed in a pocket and grabbed at a moment's notice. This was a practical solution for recording landscape views, architectural details and studies of people and nature. Such an approach was vital on tours undertaken for topographical series, where he needed to collect as many subjects as possible. During his first trip to Rome, John Soane (Younger; 1786–1823) watched Turner making 'rough pencil sketches to the astonishment of the Fashionables' and asked why he only drew in pencil instead of watercolour, to which 'he grunted for answer that it would take up too much time to colour in the open air – he could make 15 or 16 pencil sketches to one coloured'.[40]

Across sequences of pages in these books can be found a continual progress of rapid notation-style sketches, described by one observer as 'a kind of shorthand' or 'writing rather than drawing'.[41] Alongside the smaller books Turner used a variety of other formats including books of a medium size, often used for full-page or double-spread on-the-spot composition studies of subjects he might later develop in watercolour. These demonstrate a tighter handling of the pencil, with precise and accurate details of architecture and natural formations. Turner used wider books for panoramic views, or drew across two pages, sometimes even peeling back the edge of one or more leaves to continue on further pages when he ran out of space. On several trips he made use of larger soft-covered books that could be rolled up into a pocket. Turner carried one sketchbook in each of these four formats during his aforementioned Meuse, Moselle and Rhine tour in 1824, each being used for different purposes[42] – a method he found so convenient that he repeated it the following year.[43] Thus during an 1825 tour of Holland, when he visited Cologne to make sketches for his companion to the *Harbour of Dieppe*, he used the small but fat *Holland* sketchbook (CCXIV, Tate, London; cat. 2.2) for quick records and a slightly larger, horizontal-format *Holland, Meuse and Cologne* book (CCXV, Tate, London) for more expansive sketches, often over two pages.

The watercolours or oil paintings Turner produced in his studio can usually be traced back to one or several sketches, though the raw material was manipulated and combined with memory and imagination to reach its final form. In the case of *Harbour of Dieppe: Changement de Domicile* (cat. 1), no single sketch contained the visual data that Turner needed, so he made use of a number of drawings for his composition. Art historians Martin Butlin and Evelyn Joll have identified five specific sketches that contain elements incorporated into the final painting, but it is likely that he used many more than that.[44] The general view is provided by a full-page sketch in the *Rivers Meuse and Moselle* sketchbook that gives a highly generalised sense of the harbour's shape, with the surrounding buildings roughly blocked in alongside quick vertical lines for masts and some shading (fig. 15). Turner had to consult other pages of the book for more specific details such as the Hôtel d'Anvers, the architecture of which he carefully recorded with colour notes (D19989); the tower and dome of the Church of Saint-Jacques (D19996); shipping (D20000); and the people that crowd the quay (for example, D19983 and D19994; all Tate, London). Few of these fragments are reproduced literally – rather, they provide a sense of the place, which Turner then reimagined in the final painting infused with golden light.

Despite the dominance of pencil-only drawings in Turner's sketchbooks, he did sometimes use wash, watercolour, ink and chalk while sketching on tour, although it can be difficult to determine what was done in front of the motif and what was added later in his lodgings or back in the studio. On his 1824 trip, for example, he prepared one side of each of the pages in his *Moselle (or Rhine)* (CCXIX) and *Trèves and Rhine* (CCXVIII; both Tate, London) sketchbooks with a grey wash to create a mid-tone. He then drew outlines and shading in pencil and used white chalk and the techniques of scratching through or blotting out the wash to achieve highlights. In this way he was able to record tonal studies of the landscape on the spot with minimal equipment or add further effects with additional washes later. Four pages of the *Trèves and Rhine* book are executed in the same palette of watercolour and gouache, suggesting he worked them all up together over previously sketched pencil outlines once he was back in his lodgings.[45] Occasionally he painted directly in watercolour while travelling, especially when he encountered landscapes, natural features, local dress and customs for the first time. Thus, on his first Italian tour he used watercolour in two sketchbooks to respond to the landscapes at various locations, such as the view of San Giorgio Maggiore in Venice (fig. 25). The spontaneity of handling evident in this work, the specificity of the early morning light over the water, and its difference from Turner's later Venetian watercolours all point to it having been painted directly from the subject, rather than based on pencil sketches.[46]

Turner returned to direct watercolour painting during trips to Switzerland between 1841 and 1844, made after he had stopped working for topographical publishers. No longer obliged to collect as many subjects as possible, he was free to spend hours sitting comfortably at his hotel room window, using pure watercolour to capture the momentary effects of light from across the lake at different times of day and in all weathers. While some of the resulting pictures are clearly private exercises, others, like his studies for the famous *Rigi* series of watercolours, served a commercial purpose, being presented by his agent Thomas Griffith (1795–1868) as samples for pictures that were available for commission.

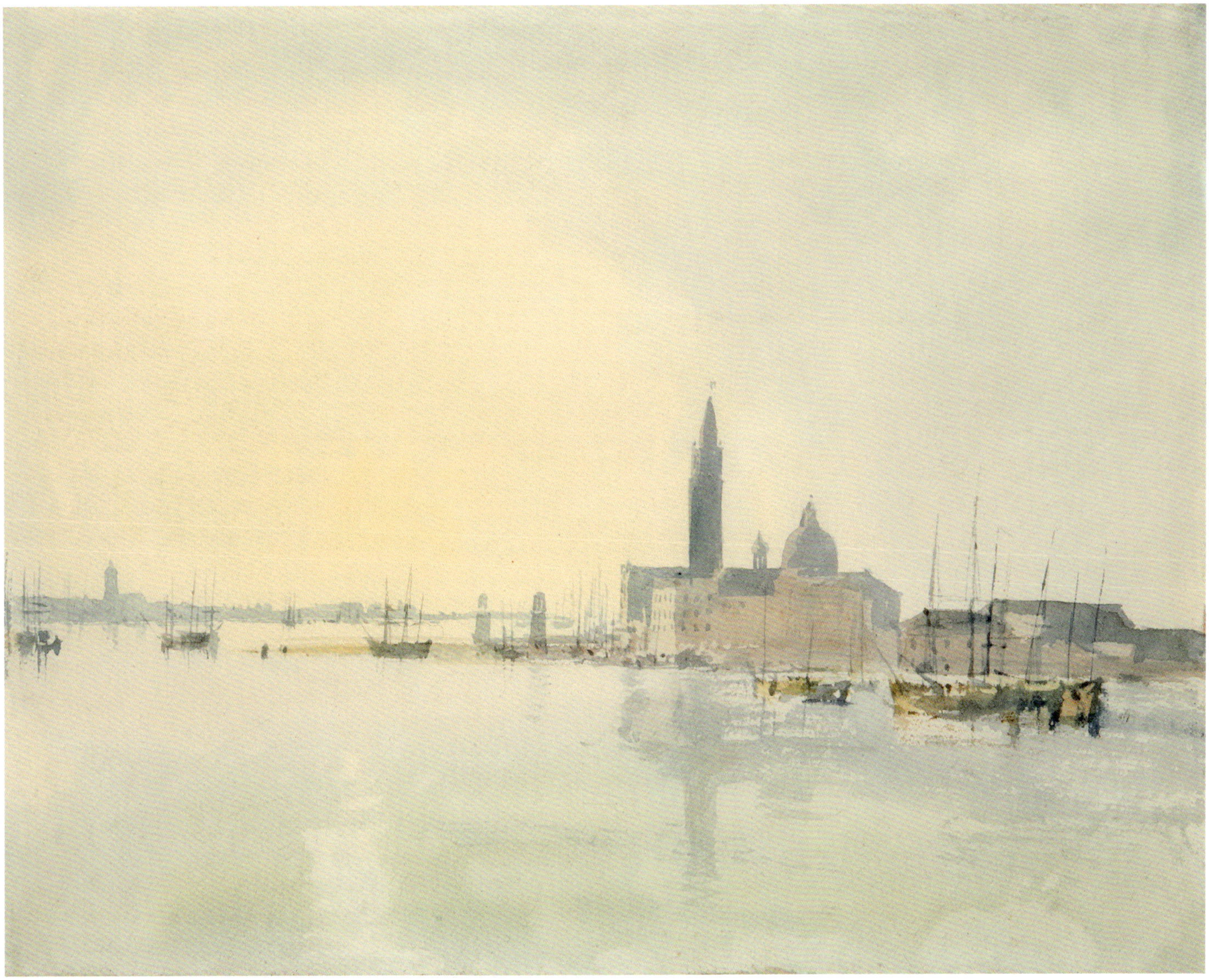

25 *Venice: San Giorgio Maggiore – Early Morning*, 1819, *Como and Venice* sketchbook, watercolour on paper, 22.3 × 28.7 cm, Tate, London (D15254; CLXXXI 4)

Turner used both pencil and watercolour during his final trip, a holiday to Boulogne in May 1845 that he described as a flight 'from Town to revival from a little change of air'.[47] These, his final tour sketches, reflect his continuing fascination with observing the effects of light on cliffs, beaches, water and air, all captured with boldness of colour and freedom of brush. Pure fantasy creeps into one of his studies, an image of a harpooned whale thrashing in waves and blood (fig. 26).[48] Turner never saw such a sight himself, relying instead on his recollection of engravings to complete his study of the sea. Yet the picture served a purpose, as he was at this time engaged in a series of four oil paintings with whaling subjects. Even on his final holiday and at the age of 70, Turner was using the experience of travel to fire his imagination for potential paintings.

THE ROMANTIC TRAVELLER BECOMES THE 'BRIGHT-EYED MARINER'

The most convincing description we have of Turner the traveller in the 1830s is also largely a work of invention. It was provided by the writer Leitch Ritchie (1800–1865), who penned the commentary for the three *Annual Tour* publications. The title is a play on words, referring both to the artist's yearly expeditions and to the volumes themselves, which take the form of the then popular yearbook anthologies known as 'annuals'. Decoding the pun reveals the trick of the narrative, which is that Ritchie constructed stories of three coherent tours from the series of views Turner made as the result of at least five separate visits to France over the previous decade. Ritchie was living in Normandy at this time, and probably travelled along the Loire and Seine alone.[49] Although he never actually claims to have been accompanied by Turner, he gives his account in the first person plural. His descriptions of the artist sketching, invitations to stand in his shoes and the welcoming bonhomie of his narrative, together with the engravings, encourage us to imagine ourselves travelling by boat, coach and foot through France with the artist and writer. While Turner is therefore rarely described directly, he is nevertheless constantly invoked by the authorial 'we' into which author, artist and reader merge as the single figure of the Romantic traveller.

This 'annual tourist' is an urbane and professional modern gentleman: an 'intellectual traveller' who has graduated from his Grand Tour and formative early adventures to make travel a way of life. Upon visiting (or reading about) different locations, he is capable of calling to mind 'moral and historical associations' that elevate his perception of the landscape as he witnesses it, turning it into a poem or painting before his eyes.[50] His sensorial experience of the landscape is constantly supplemented by the imagination, just as 'the poetical imagination of our friend [Turner] has so characteristically supplied' the human details of his landscape and architectural views.[51] At one point, walking between Beaugency and Blois, the sensations 'steep our senses in a kind of intoxication' as the narrator imagines treading the same ground in centuries past as a 'knight-errant!' The passage is comically quixotic, as he has been forced to walk after the mishap of missing the coach. His discomfort, however, is alleviated by 'the advantages of imagination … we will continue to fill up the dreary waste which life sometimes presents with the airy fabrics of poetry'.[52] The artistic imagination is thus presented here as a sort of game – a strategy to overcome the inevitable disappointments of the modern world, which so often fails to live up to the expectations of the intellectual traveller.

As Turner's restless touring schedule came to an end in the second half of the 1840s, the artist continued to imagine himself as a (mis)adventuring traveller. Indeed, the feats of courage he recounted grew in inverse proportion to the dangers he actually encountered as he swapped gruelling touring for gentler holiday trips in his old age. In the full title of *Snow Storm – Steam-Boat off a Harbour's Mouth* (1842), Turner

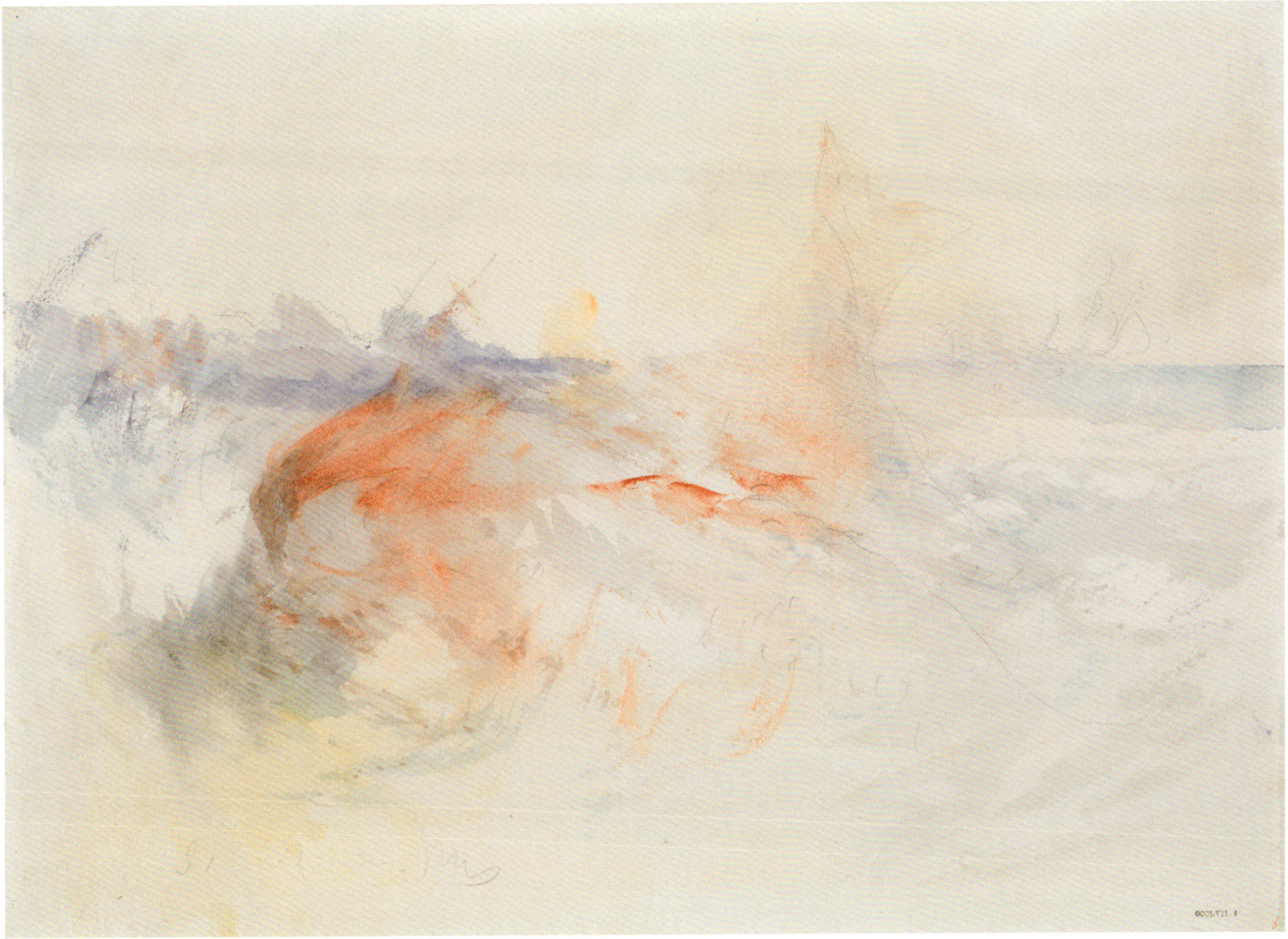

26 *A Harpooned Whale*, 1845, *Ambleteuse and Wimereux* sketchbook, graphite and watercolour on paper, 23.8 × 33.6 cm, Tate, London (D35391; CCCLVII 6)

(OVERLEAF) Detail of cat. 1

states, 'The Author was in this Storm on the Night the *Ariel* left Harwich'; he later claimed, 'I got the sailors to lash me to the mast to observe it; I was lashed for four hours, and I did not expect to escape, but I felt bound to record it if I did.'[53] This anecdote, recalling a similar story told about the French marine painter Claude-Joseph Vernet, is usually assumed to be an invention.[54] But it is revealing of how Turner's self-image as a travelling artist transfigured into the alter ego he adopted in his final years, when he was confined to making regular visits to Margate to stay with the boarding-house keeper from whom he took his pseudonym. Captain (or Admiral) Booth – as he was known in Chelsea, where he kept a secret home on the Thames with Mrs Sophia Booth – was imagined by locals to be a retired mariner, owing to his habit of surveying the Thames and the sky above it through a telescope from his balcony. Confined to dry land, Turner never stopped looking to the horizon. Like Samuel Taylor Coleridge's *Ancient Mariner*, he felt compelled to relive his adventures in his mind, thus embodying a new version of the artist-traveller who continued to range restlessly across land, sea and sky even while his feet remained planted by his fireside in London.

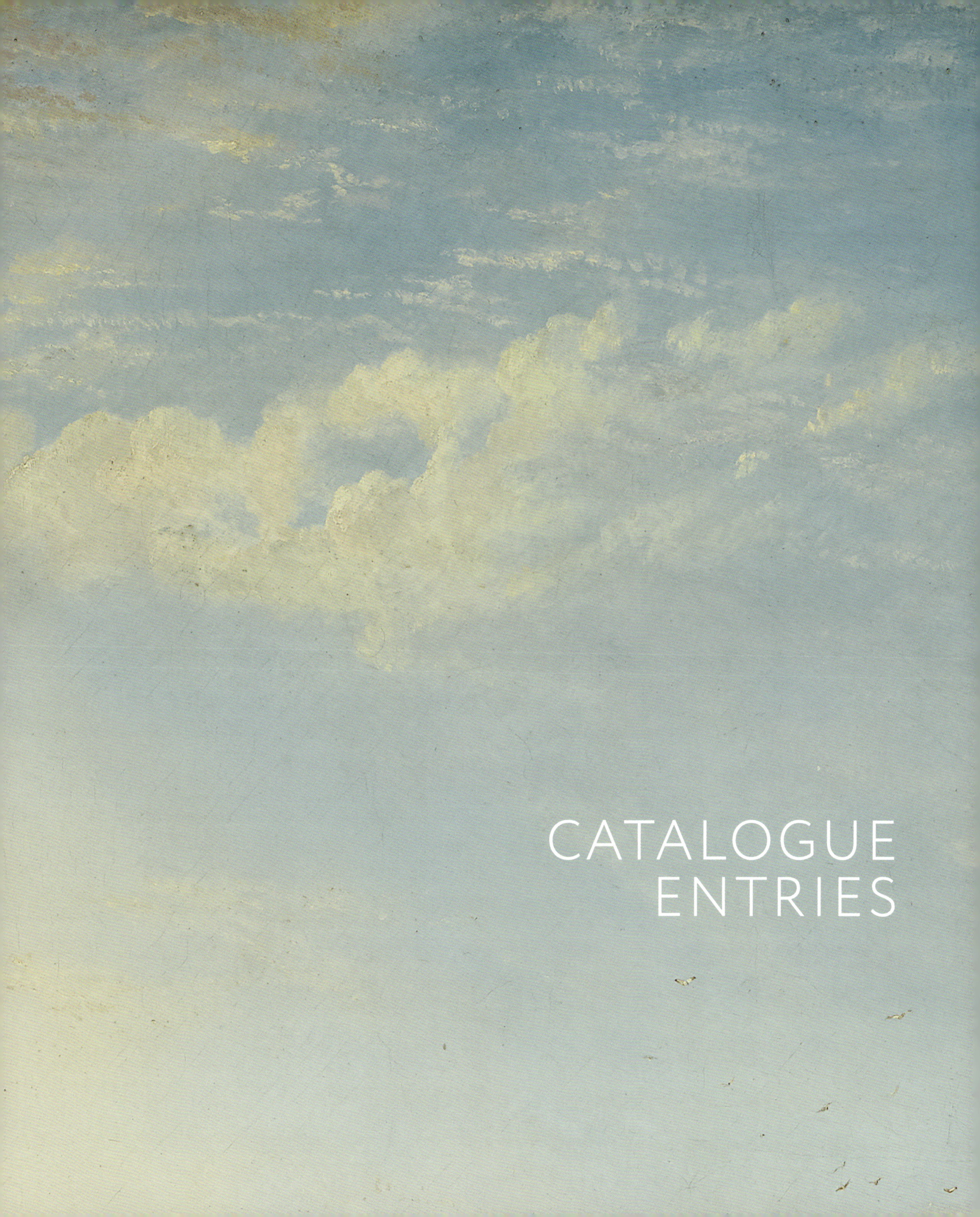

CATALOGUE ENTRIES

1

Joseph Mallord William Turner (1775–1851)

HARBOUR OF DIEPPE: CHANGEMENT DE DOMICILE

Exhibited 1825, but subsequently dated 1826
Oil on canvas
173.7 × 225.4 cm
The Frick Collection, New York
Henry Clay Frick Bequest 1914.1.122

After his first visit to Dieppe in 1821, Turner returned in 1824 to the French coastal city, situated across the English Channel from Brighton, at the end of a tour of the Netherlands and Germany.[1] Over two days, 11 and 12 September, he produced some 60 sketches of the city and its inhabitants. Back in his London studio a few days later, he set his sights on creating a monumental harbour scene, his second since his 1818 canvas, *Dort or Dordrecht: The Dort Packet-Boat from Rotterdam becalmed* (fig. 1). For *Dieppe*, Turner selected a view looking south-west, down the Quai Henri IV on the right side of the canvas, teeming with people and moored boats. Eighteenth-century buildings line the quay, including the impressive Hôtel d'Anvers (cat. 1.6), with its triangular pediment and double-storey pilasters (the city had been nearly destroyed by Anglo-Dutch bombardment in 1694, during the Nine Years' War).[2] Many of Turner's sketches made on site inform the composition (fig. 15), though in the painting he exaggerated elements like the height of buildings and eliminated cross streets. In the distance, hazy under the white sun, appear the tower and dome of Saint-Jacques (cats 1.1 and 1.3). The island of Le Pollet, home to a community of fishermen, features at far left. Its inhabitants, like the couple on the quay in red headdresses discoursing over a pot and packages (cat. 1.4), are identifiable by their traditional clothing, which Turner also studied in sketches. The couple

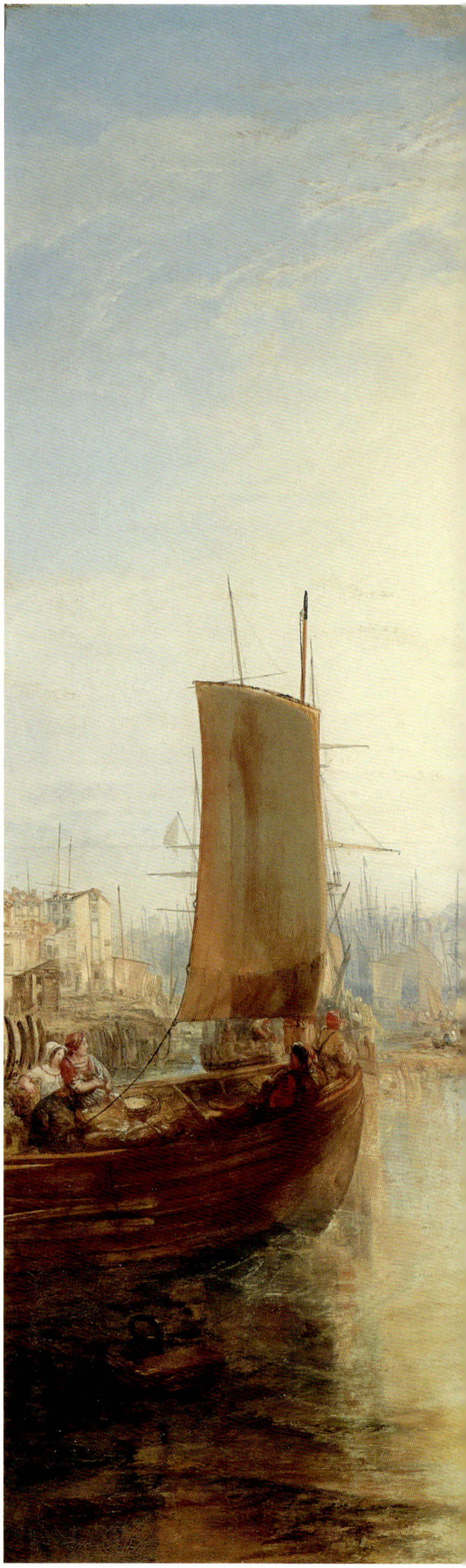

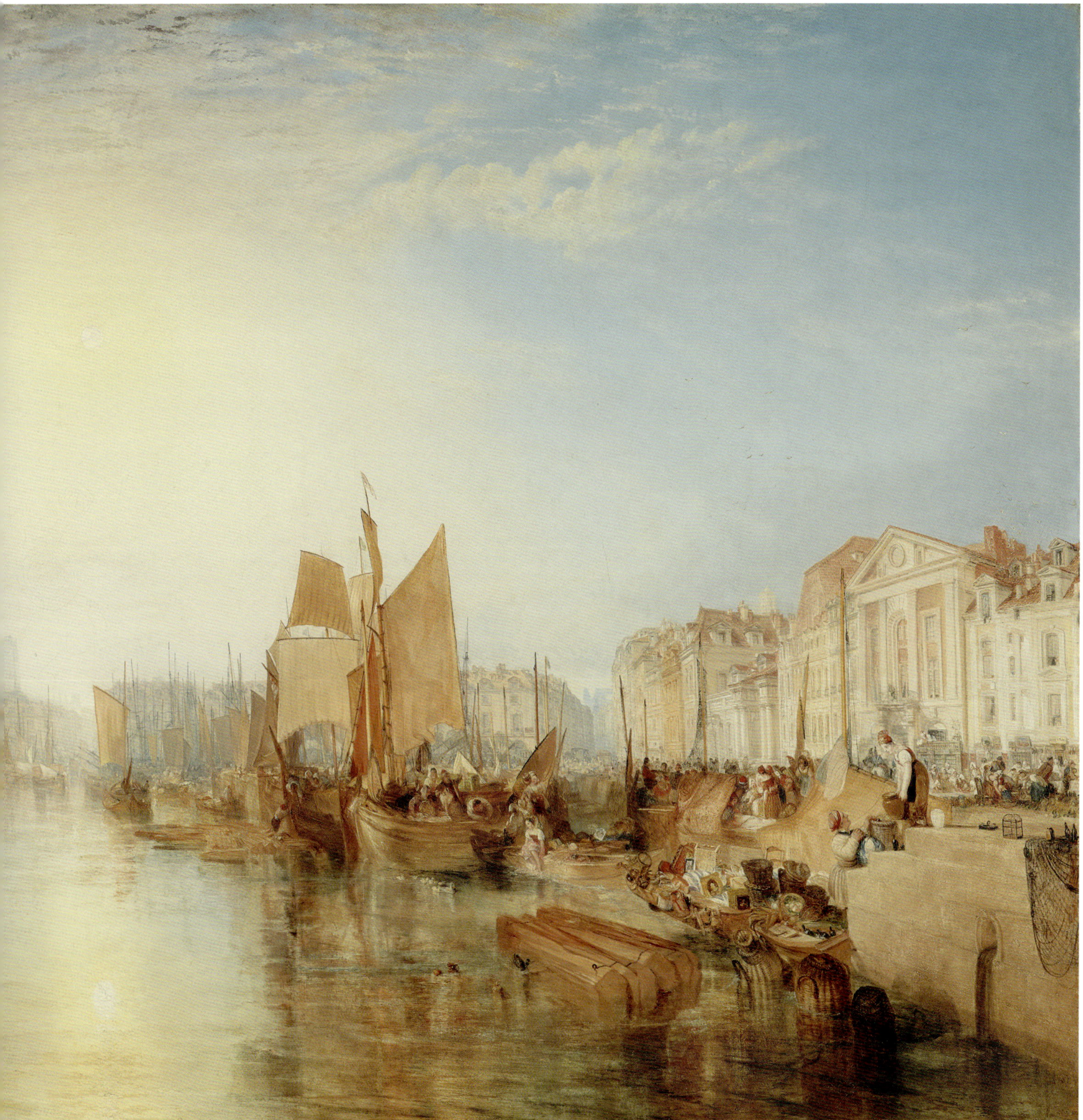

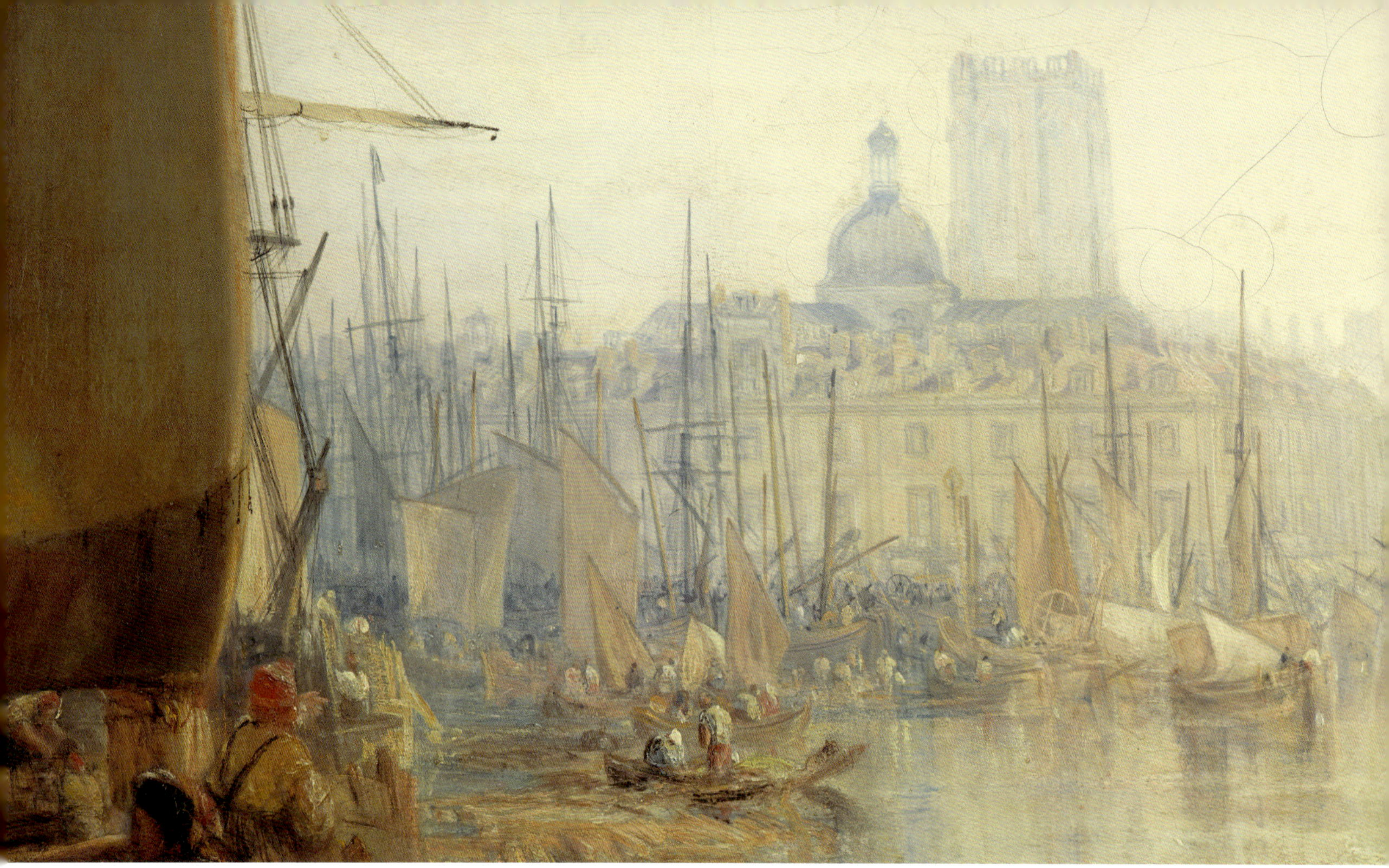

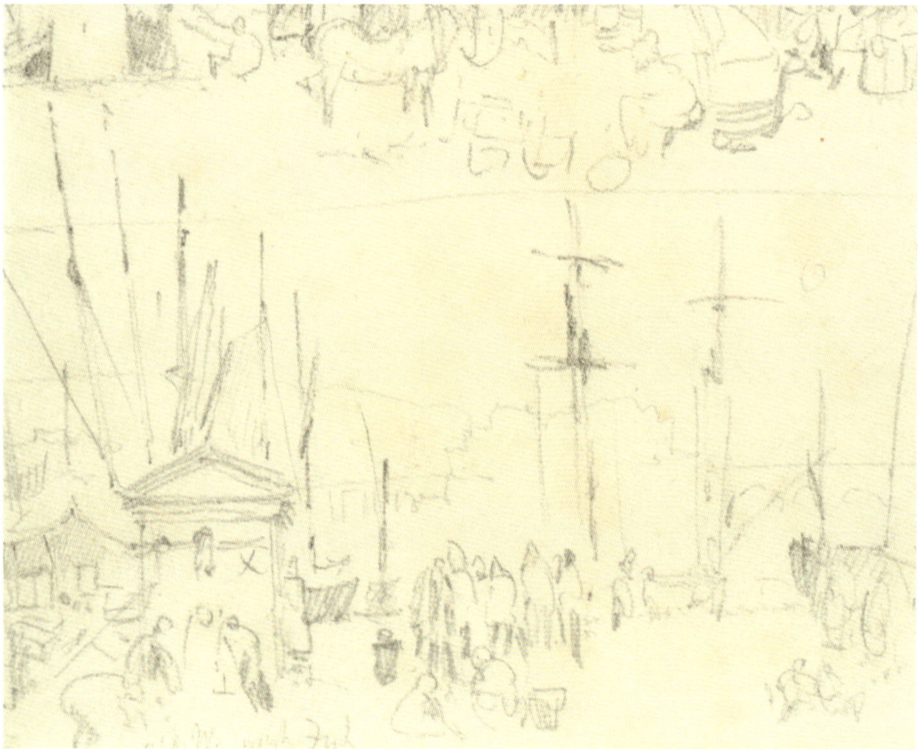

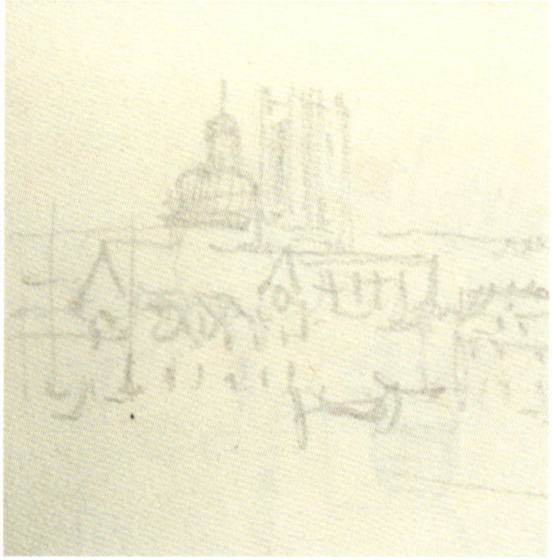

1.1 (TOP) The tower and dome of Saint-Jacques

1.2 (LEFT) *Sketches of the Harbour and Beach at Dieppe* (detail), 1821, *Dieppe, Rouen and Paris* sketchbook, graphite on paper, 12.3 × 11.8 cm, Tate, London (D24560; CCLVIII 32)

1.3 (ABOVE) Detail of fig. 15

may be unloading wares from the object-laden boat to stock the outdoor market set up in the distance behind them, where a soldier reaches up to place a framed picture on the exterior of a building. Nearby, a sign reading *Débit de Tabac* indicates a tobacconist's shop. Sails and masts pierce the soaring sky (cat. 1.2), while floating debris mingles with reflections in the water.

When Turner exhibited *Dieppe* in London at the Royal Academy Summer Exhibition of 1825, the response was mixed. Some critics lauded the composition, comparing it favourably to the revered landscapes of the seventeenth-century French artist Claude. Many – including those who praised *Dieppe*'s drawing and effects – derided its colour, the honeyed tones of which were deemed inaccurate and unsuited to a city on the northern coast of France. One commentator

1.4 The inhabitants of Le Pollet on the quay

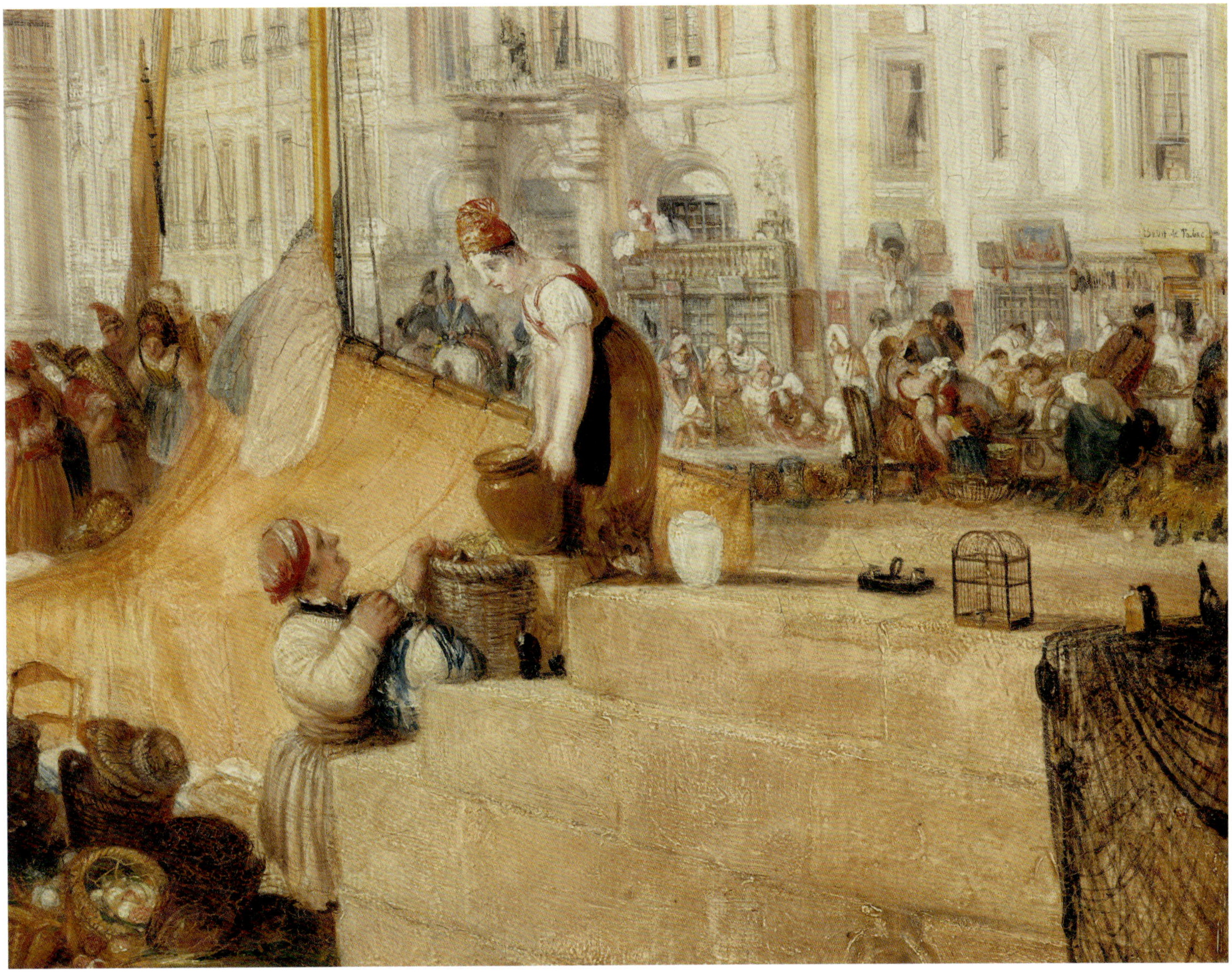

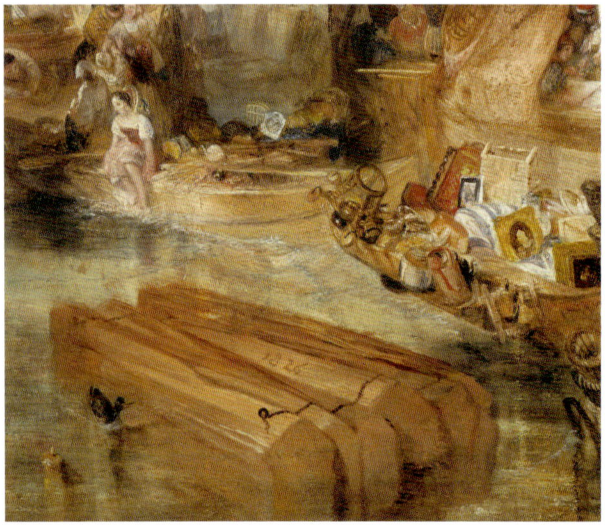

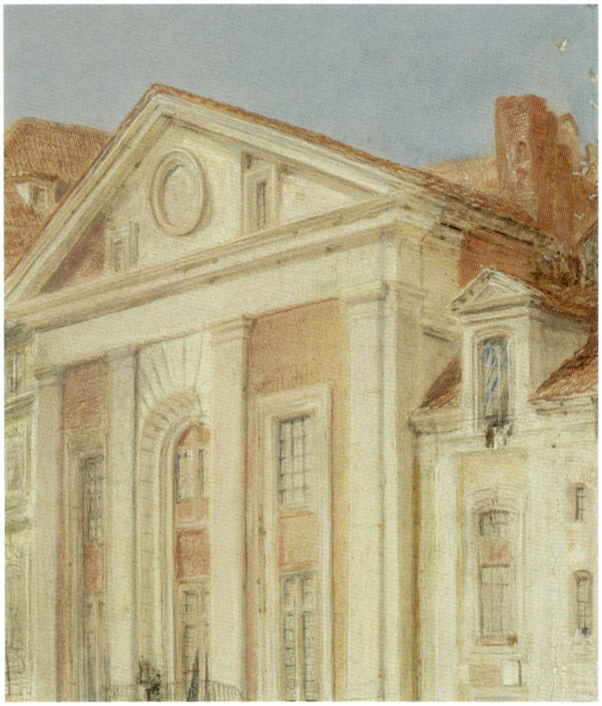

delighted in Turner's 'magnificent view' but could not reconcile his colours with reality: 'But we know Dieppe,' he wrote, 'and can't easily clothe it in such fairy hues.'[3] The comments were consistent with critical response to Turner's works over the years, which came more and more to lament what was seen as his increasingly unnatural colouring, while continuing to celebrate his unrivalled skill.

Turner inscribed the painting's French subtitle, *Changement de domicile* ('change of home address'), on a piece of wood floating in the lower left corner (now barely legible, possibly painted over by the artist). Precisely what the subtitle refers to remains obscure.[4] It suits the bustling life in the harbour, which evokes a sense of movement and transition, the outdoor market full of goods seeking new homes. He also added a date on the logs floating near the boat laden with home wares (cat. 1.5). Though the last digit is difficult to decipher, close examination has shown that it most likely reads *1826*. The artist may have continued to work on the painting after its exhibition in 1825 – not uncommon for Turner or his contemporaries – and signed it the following year.

It is unclear when *Dieppe* was acquired by its first owner, a John Broadhurst who has yet to be firmly identified among several men of that name recorded in England at this time.[5] He disposed of it and its companion piece of the following year (cat. 2), as well as a third, earlier, Turner landscape, at auction in July 1828.[6] The paintings were reportedly bought in – retained by the auction house – at a lower price than he had initially paid for them.[7] One John Broadhurst of Macclesfield, Cheshire, was a silk manufacturer who was registered as bankrupt on 20 June 1828, weeks before the sale.[8] It may have also been for Broadhurst that in 1827 Turner began a third monumental port scene, *The Harbour of Brest: The Quayside and Château* (Tate, London). He left it unfinished, likely abandoning it when Broadhurst divested himself of his Turners in 1828.

Dieppe and *Cologne* were subsequently sold to the London art collector James Wadmore (1782–1853), from whose posthumous sale in 1854 they were acquired for the Liverpool banker and collector John Naylor (1813–1889). In 1914, in the first months of the First World War, they entered the collection of Henry Clay Frick in New York.

1.5 (TOP) Date inscribed on floating logs

1.6 (BOTTOM) The Hôtel d'Anvers with its triangular pediment and double-storey pilasters

1.7 (OPPOSITE) Moored boats on Quai Henri IV

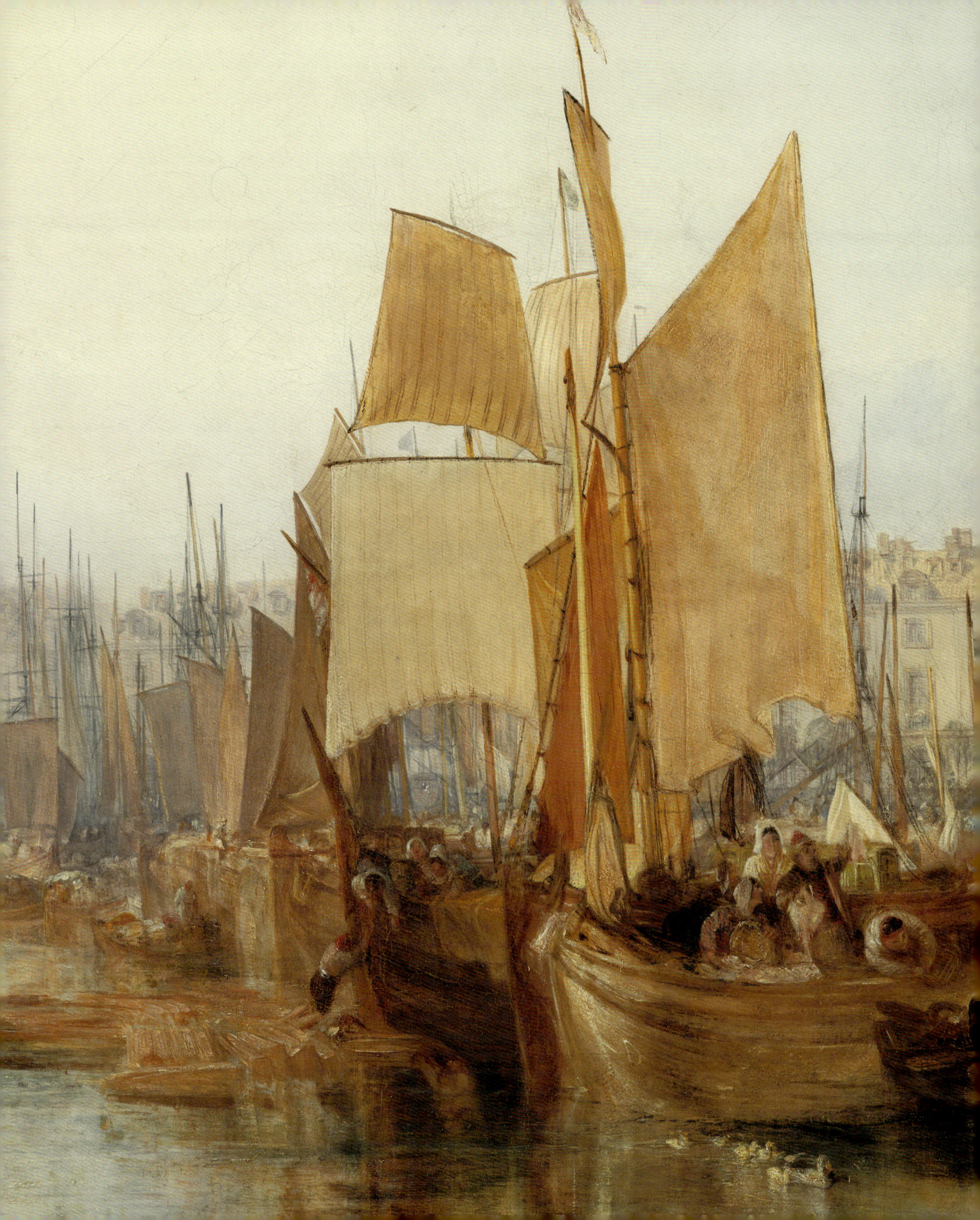

2

Joseph Mallord William Turner (1775–1851)

COLOGNE, THE ARRIVAL OF A PACKET-BOAT: EVENING

1826
Oil on canvas
168.6 × 224.2 cm
The Frick Collection, New York
Henry Clay Frick Bequest 1914.1.119

In August 1825, having installed *Dieppe* (cat. 1) earlier that season at the Royal Academy Summer Exhibition, Turner departed for a tour of the Netherlands that would also take him on his third visit to Cologne, one of the oldest cities in Germany and an entry point along the river Rhine for British travellers on the Grand Tour.[1] At this point he may have already planned to make a companion piece to *Dieppe*; his travels through the Netherlands suggest that he sought a Dutch subject.[2] His stop in Cologne at the end of this trip, however, set the course for his next painting.

He composed a view of Cologne looking south down the Rhine with the city, at right, protected behind its medieval walls. During his visits between 1817 and 1825 he had made numerous sketches of the city, its buildings and its port from different viewpoints, and for this painting he turned to architectural elements and perspectives that initially caught his eye in 1817. His earliest known sketch of the city (fig. 14) studied a similar view as the Frick painting: the dominating tower of the twelfth-century Groß St Martin's church (cat. 2.1); below it the arched Rhine Gate (cat. 2.2), leading into the heart of the city; in the distance, to the left of Groß St Martin, the sphere, spire and roof of the sixteenth-century Stapelhaus.[3] At far left is the ancient town of Deutz, connected to Cologne across the Rhine by a then newly constructed bridge supported on a base of pontoons (cat. 2.6). Turner captures

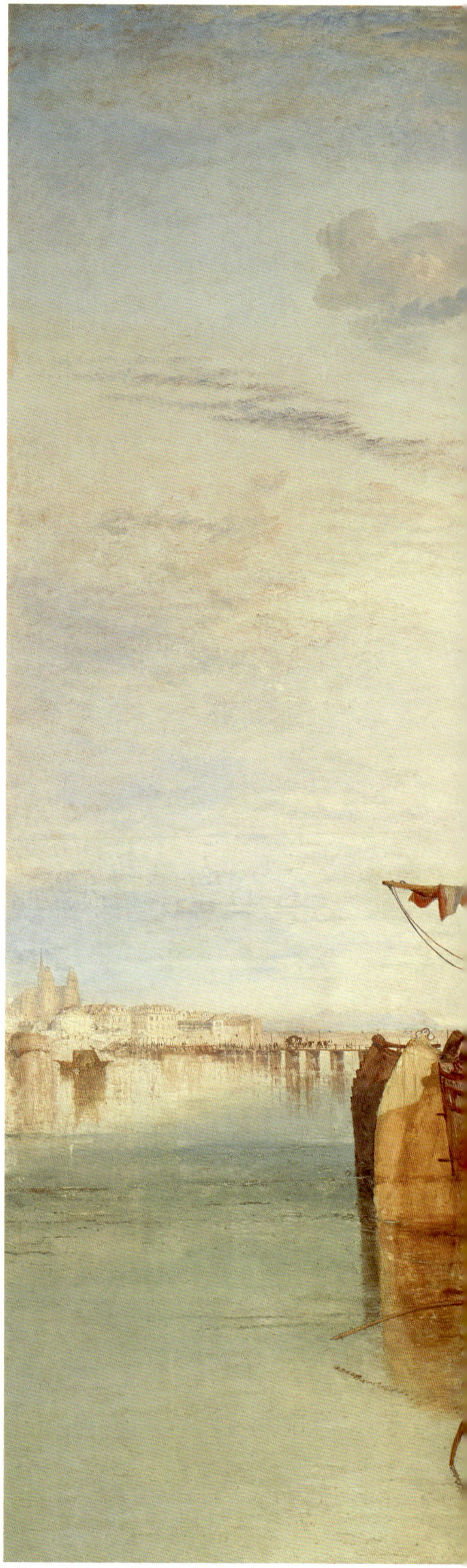

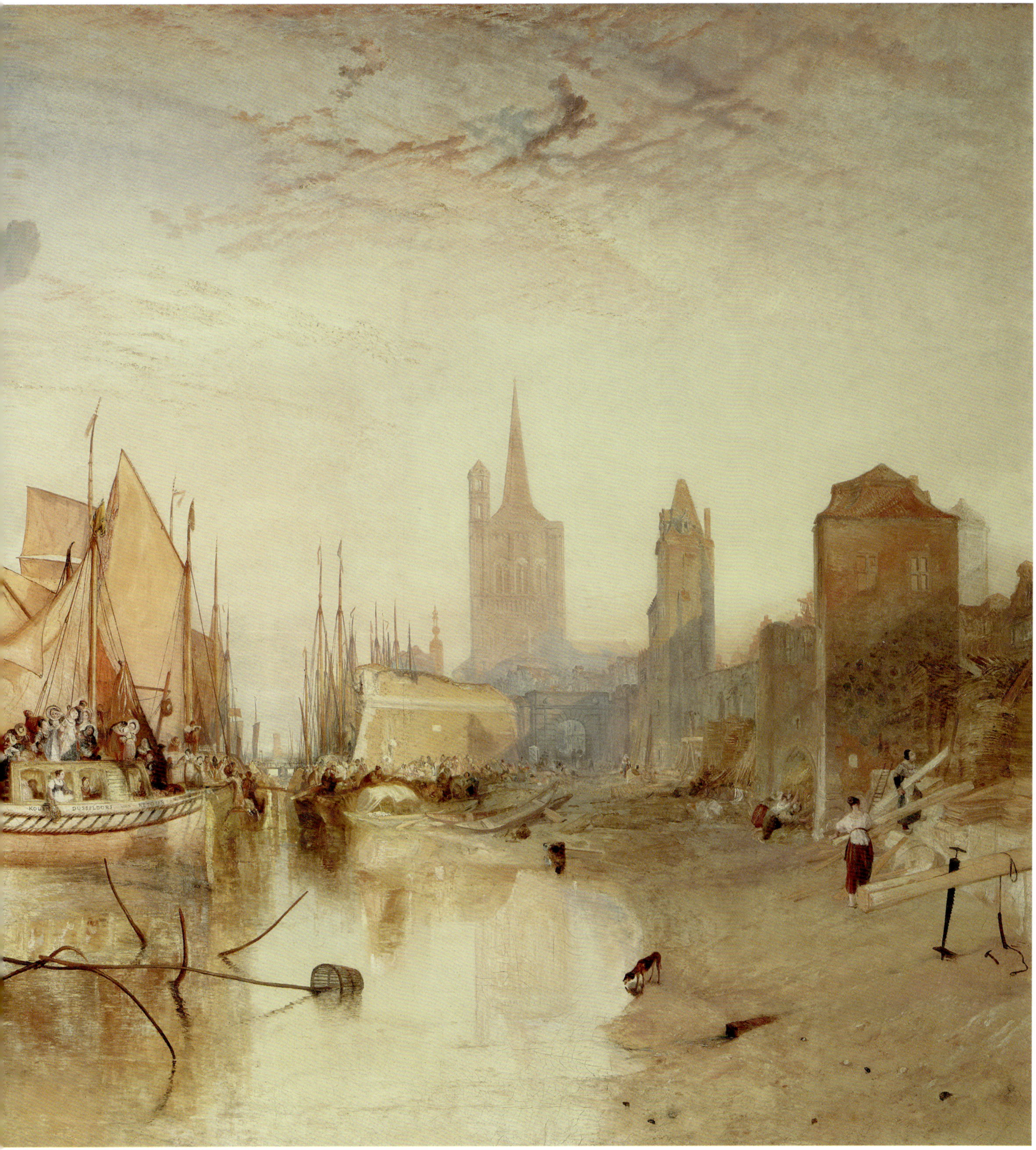

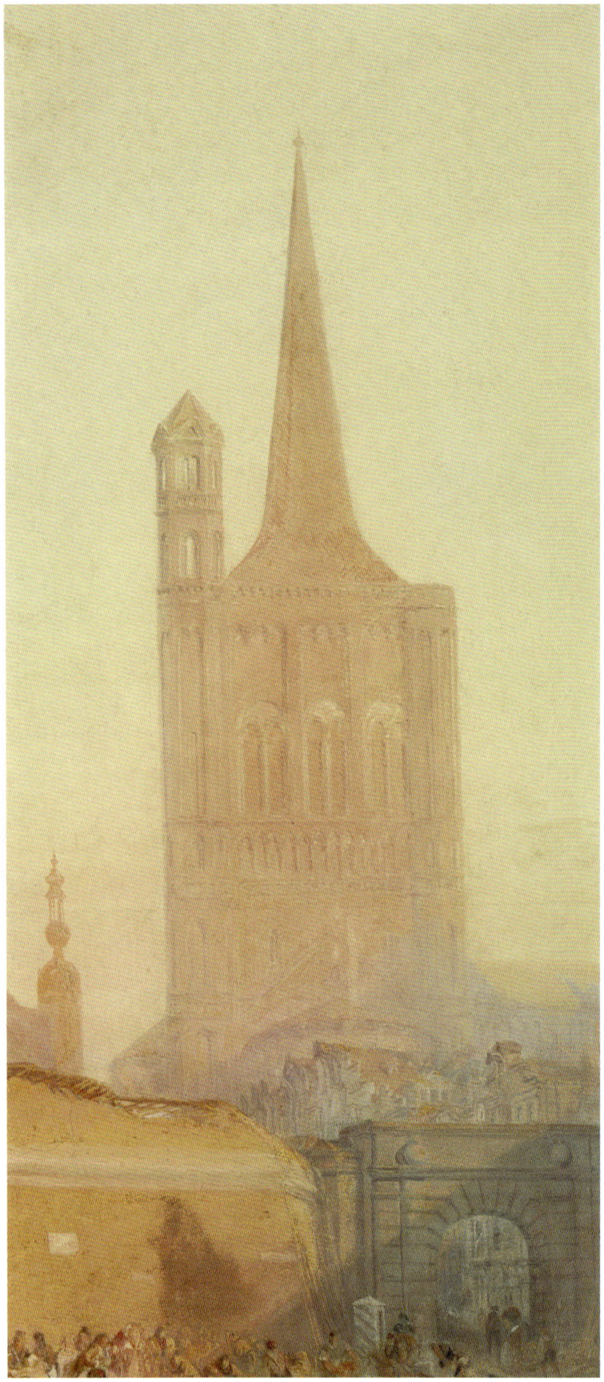

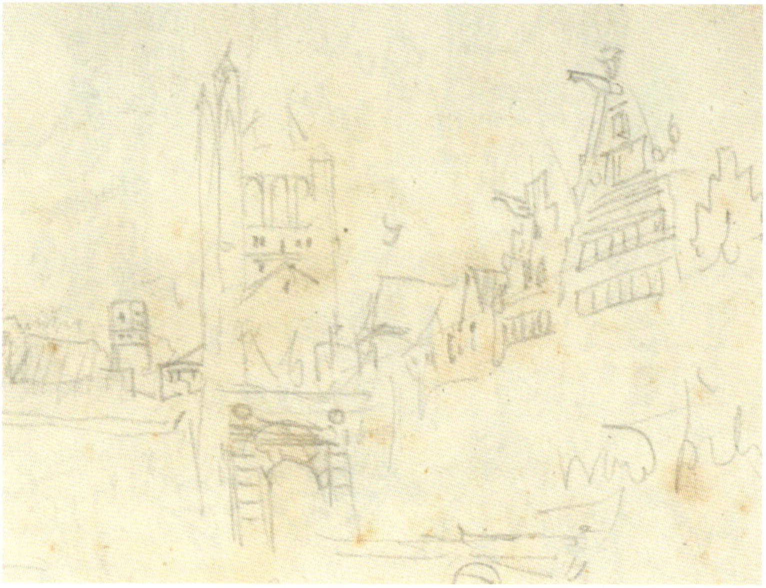

the rich architectural history of Cologne, which continued to evolve over the years of his visits. As in *Dieppe*, in *Cologne* Turner invents, edits and augments the city's features to suit his interests, adding and eliminating elements and retaining the historic appearance of edifices that had changed dramatically by the time he was painting; the peaked tower of the medieval Frankenturm, for example, to the right of Groß St Martin, had been diminished to half its height by 1823, and the tower at far right, the Trankgassentor, was demolished in 1825.[4] Cologne's most famous building, its cathedral, lies outside Turner's view, though the shadow on the packet boat at centre may be cast by one of the cathedral's twin spires in the evening sun.

The heart of the composition – like *Dieppe* – is the harbour itself and the spectacle of its water, boats and life. The spindly, broken form of abandoned fishing equipment occupies the foreground, where a lean dog laps water near a spout dispelling waste (cat. 2.5). The painting's title refers to the ferry at centre, inscribed *KOLEN DUSSELDORF UND RETOUR* ('Cologne Düsseldorf and Return'; cat. 2.3), perplexingly misspelling Cologne's German name (Koeln or Köln). The use of *retour* ('return'), sometimes interpreted as French, is more likely to be the Dutch term with the same meaning; the packet boat's Dutch point of origin – where it will return from these German stops – is also suggested by the red, white and blue *Statenvlag* (state flag) of the Netherlands hanging on the boom. Turner may have taken such a ferry from the Netherlands to Cologne. On the stern, below the flag, appears the word *AMITIE* (*amitié*, French for 'friendship'), which has been variously interpreted by scholars in contexts as wide as Turner's personal friendships and an ironic reference to Napoleon's occupation of Cologne. It was a common name for a vessel and remains so today.

2.1 (LEFT) The tower of Groß St Martin above the Rhine Gate

2.2 (RIGHT) *The Rhine Gate, Cologne* (detail), 1825, *Holland* sketchbook, graphite on paper, 15.5 × 9.5 cm, Tate, London (D19122; CCXIV 143)

2.3 (OPPOSITE) The packet boat

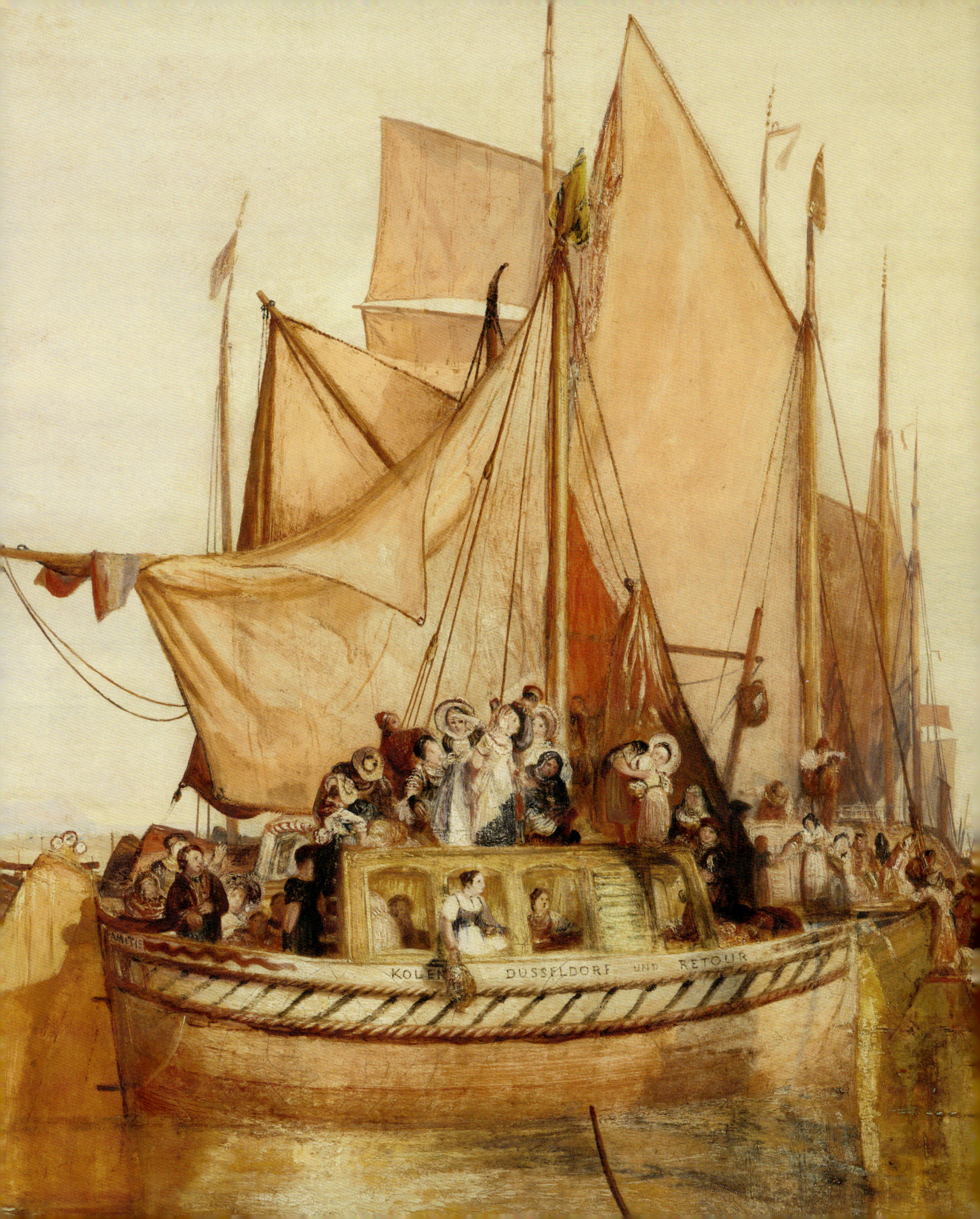
AMITIE
KOLEN
DUSSELDORF UND RETOUR

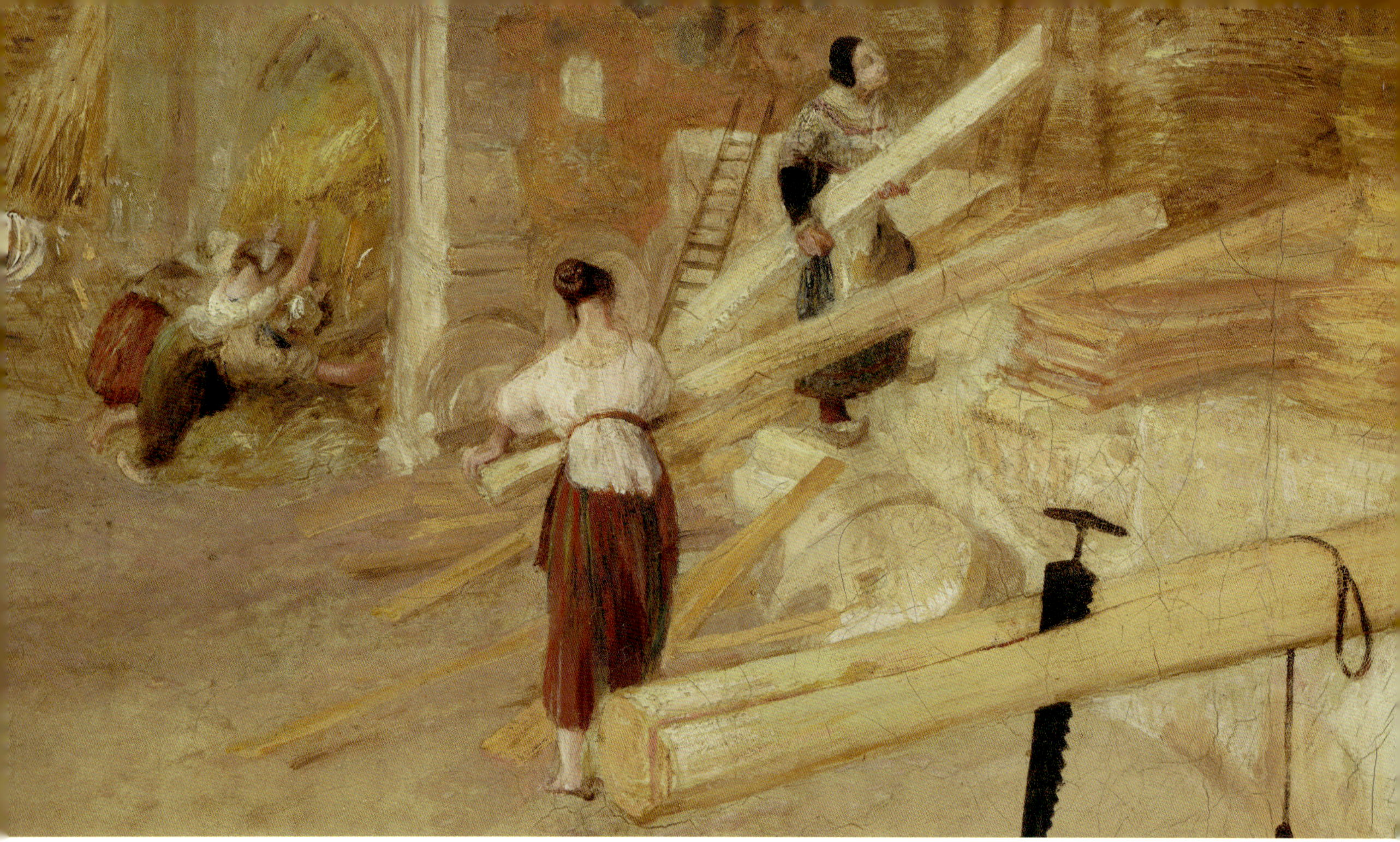

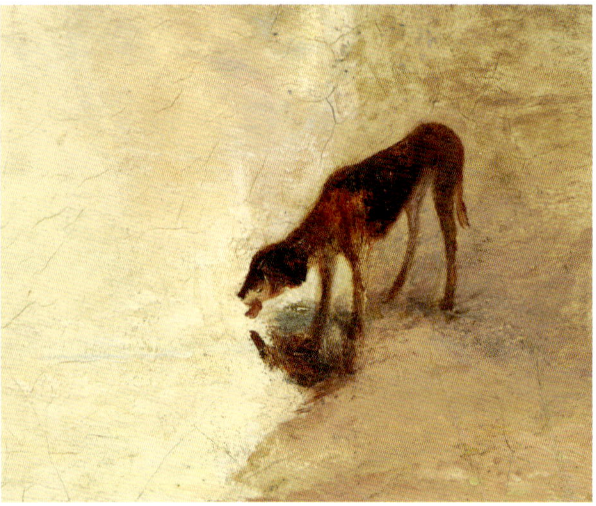

2.4 (TOP) Working women on the shore

2.5 (BOTTOM) Dog on the shore

The packet boat is loaded predominantly with women, many of them looking towards the shore, where another group of women work, lifting lumber and stuffing hay (cat. 2.4). Through these figures Turner introduces tensions of social class, with a number of well-dressed women on the boat representing travel and leisure, and those on land the working poor. The predominance of female figures in Turner's scene of arrival has been connected to the legend of Saint Ursula, the fourth-century saint who travelled with 11,000 virgin women in her retinue; arriving in Cologne, they were massacred by the Huns.[5] The fifth-century church of St Ursula, one of Cologne's most visited sites, contains the Goldene Kammer (Golden Chamber), a room decorated with the alleged remains – thousands of bones and skulls – of Ursula and her followers. A celebrated painting of the subject by Claude (*Seaport with the Embarkation of Saint Ursula*, 1641) had in 1824 been purchased by the British government from the collection of John Julius Angerstein to form part of the nucleus of the National Gallery.

Exhibited in the Summer Exhibition of 1826, *Cologne* was still in Turner's possession a year later, when, in August 1827, he wrote to his father (who assisted the artist for much of his career): 'Mr Broadhurst is to have the Picture of Cologne.'[6] The length of time between exhibition and acquisition may preclude the theory that

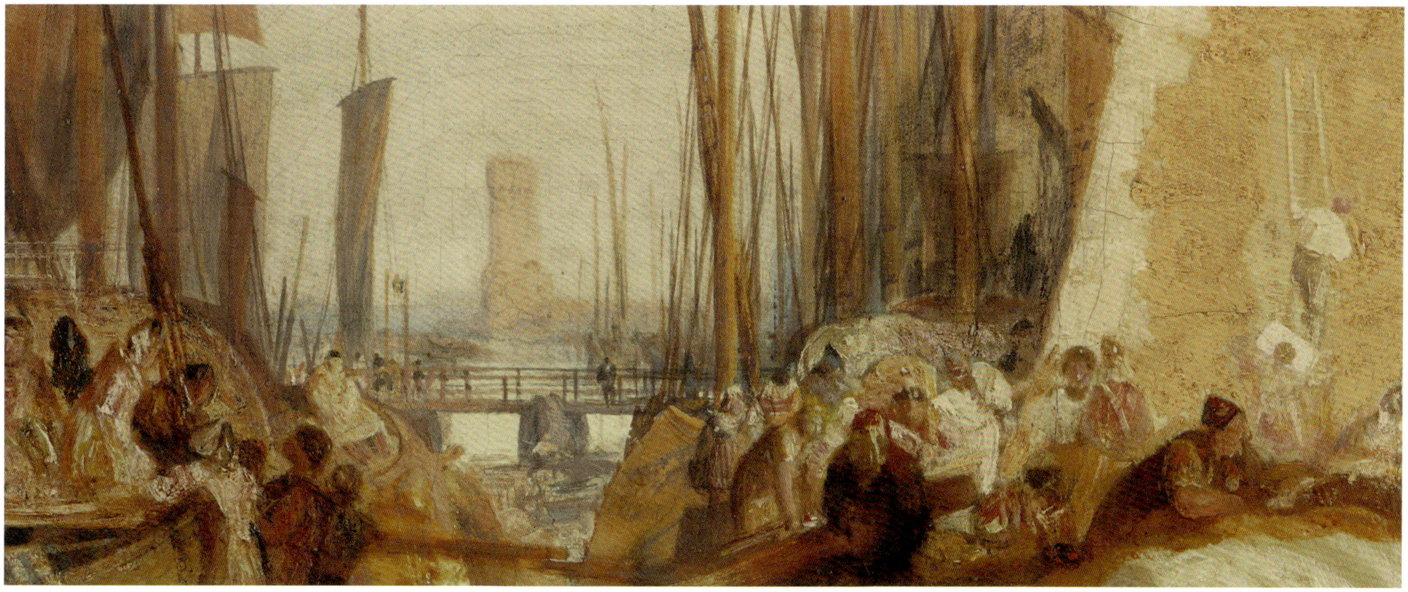

2.6 Bridge, supported on a base of pontoons, connecting Cologne to Deutz

Broadhurst commissioned *Dieppe* and *Cologne*. With this reference to the picture's mysterious first owner, Turner also warns of the painting's delicate physical state. 'But you must not by any means wet it,' he continues, 'for all the colour will come off ... it must not be touched with Water or Varnish (only wiped with a silk handkerchief) until I return.' The precise condition of the painting at that point is unknown, though recent examination confirmed that both *Dieppe* and *Cologne* are painted in oils and not with water-soluble materials, a rumour initiated by early accounts.[7] Other such second-hand reports – which certainly cannot always be trusted – include one by John Ruskin, who recounted that during the Summer Exhibition Turner coated the painting with lampblack to tone down its colour out of consideration for portraits by Sir Thomas Lawrence displayed on either side, which it was overpowering.[8] Critics still derided Turner's heavy use of yellow in the painting, one suggesting that his sails in *Cologne* 'might not be inappropriate for Cleopatra's golden vessel'.[9]

After *Dieppe* and *Cologne* were exhibited in Knoedler's New York gallery in January 1914, Henry Clay Frick purchased *Cologne* in June of that year (*Dieppe* had apparently been sent to another potential buyer).[10] Over the summer, both were cleaned in London. When it came time to deliver Frick's *Cologne* in the autumn, Knoedler sent *Dieppe* along with it – *Dieppe* having failed to sell to the other buyer – and installed both in the newly constructed Frick mansion at 1 East 70th Street, New York, carefully covering them to protect them from dust, as the house was not yet finished. When the Frick family moved into the house in November of that year, the two Turners were already installed in the North and South Halls, presumably to satisfying effect: Frick also purchased *Dieppe* a few weeks later.

NOTES

JOURNEYS OLD AND NEW: TURNER IN THE 1820s

Christine Riding

The most comprehensive published analysis focusing on Turner's *Dieppe* and *Cologne* and other seaport paintings is New York 2017.

1. London 2013, pp. 11–19, 25–35, 103–29.
2. Quoted in Egerton 1998, p. 264.
3. Wine 2001, pp. 64, 82.
4. London 2013, pp. 51–4.
5. Butlin and Joll 1984, *Text* volume, p. 89.
6. London 2012, p. 70.
7. Quoted in London 2012, p. 15.
8. Quoted in Butlin and Joll 1984, *Text* volume, p. 127.
9. Ibid.
10. Ibid.
11. London 2013, pp. 63–7.
12. For the maritime-related series, see Shanes 1981.
13. Butlin and Joll 1984, *Text* volume, p. 124.
14. See the *Paris, Seine and Dieppe* sketchbook, CCXI, Tate, London.
15. See the *Rhine* sketchbook, CLVI; the *Holland*, CCXIV; and the *Holland, Meuse and Cologne*, CCXV, all Tate, London.
16. London, Minneapolis and New York 2003–4, pp. 12–27, 57, 94–9, 112.
17. Quoted in London 2013, p. 160.
18. These paintings were Turner's first open seascapes in oil for eight years, underscoring the importance of the Royal Academy exhibition of 1827 in showcasing contemporary British marine painting. Ibid., pp. 134–9.
19. Quoted in Ibid., p. 140.
20. The two Cowes Regatta paintings were acquired by the architect John Nash, who owned a small estate on the coast of East Cowes on the Isle of Wight: *The Regatta beating to Windward* (1828, Indianapolis Museum of Art) and *The Regatta starting for their Moorings* (1828, Victoria and Albert Museum, London). Butlin and Joll 1984, nos 242 and 243.
21. Butlin and Joll 1984, *Text* volume, p. 154.
22. London, Philadelphia and Minneapolis 2002, pp. 95–7.
23. Butlin and Joll 1984, *Text* volume, p. 134.
24. Quoted in Ibid., p. 167.
25. Cole's comments were recorded in his 1829 sketchbook and were directed at Turner's most recent works, including *Ulysses*. For the complete quotation, see Washington, DC, Dallas and New York 2007, p. 233.
26. The series was conceived by Cole in London, just prior to his visit to Turner's studio. New York 2018, p. 37.
27. London, Philadelphia and Minneapolis 2002, p. 102.
28. London 2012, p. 52.
29. London 2013, p. 23.
30. London 2000, p. 276.
31. London 2013, p. 242.
32. The Frick Collection Archive Department confirms that Miss Frick was at the National Gallery that day in 1909 with her mother. References to correspondence with Mr Frick signal that he did not accompany them.

TURNER AS AN ARTIST-TRAVELLER

Thomas Ardill

1. The repository of Turner's studio became the 'Turner Bequest' when his will was settled in 1856 and the works in the artist's own hand were given to the nation under the care of the National Gallery. Just 10 oil paintings remain with the Gallery. The others, along with the works on paper, are now part of the Tate Collection. See Brown 2012; Warrell 2014, pp. 7–17.
2. This can be seen by comparing Turner's often slight sketches of a subject with his very detailed oil paintings, as was the case with the *Harbour of Dieppe* (cat. 1), and by viewing pictures completed entirely from memory, like the *Funeral of Sir Thomas Lawrence* (1830, Tate, London), subtitled 'a sketch from memory'. Hawkesworth Fawkes was astonished to witness Turner create a watercolour of a man-of-war, not only because of the novel way he painted 'in a kind of frenzy', but also because of his ability to reproduce the 'exquisite minutia[e]' of the ship from memory. (Quoted in Wilton 1987, p. 114.)
3. Quoted in Wilton 1979, p. 12.
4. Reported by Thomas Unwins to Joseph Severn, 3 February 1829; in Unwins 1858, p. 240.
5. Warrell 1997, p. 31.
6. Warrell 1999, p. 45.
7. It was claimed that Turner would not show a single sketch to his travelling companion in Switzerland in 1802 (Shanes 2016, p. 228).
8. A. Fraser, 1872, quoted in Finley 1980, p. 54.
9. Lassels 1670.
10. J.M.W. Turner, *Fishermen at Sea*, 1796, oil on canvas, 91.4 × 122.2 cm (Tate, London).
11. Turner had begun travelling as a child, briefly attending schools in Brentford and Margate and living for a few months with an uncle at Sunningwell near Oxford, where he gained his earliest employment as a draughtsman under the architects Thomas Hardwick and Thomas Malton.
12. Balzaretti, Piana and Watkins 2015; London, Mannheim and Hamburg 1995–6, pp. 12–13.
13. Sweet 2012, p. 11.
14. Turner took full advantage of steamboat services and the timetables and guidebooks published to help their users. For example, see Ardill 2010 (rev. Imms 2016). During the 1830s, he embarked on numerous riverboat tours to collect views for his *Rivers of Europe* series, of which three volumes were published between 1833 and 1835.
15. Gilpin 1792, p. 41.
16. See versions at London's Victoria and Albert Museum, British Museum and Tate.
17. Butlin and Joll 1984, no. 47.
18. In actual fact, the painting owes more to a work by Claude that Turner would have seen in England or in print than it does to any of the French landscape master's paintings in the Louvre, of which Turner made no sketches. He was also mistaken about the painting's location, which was based on his view of Tournus, 20 miles from Mâcon (Hill 1992, p. 28).

19. Wilton 2013.
20. See Wilton 1981 and Riding and Llewellyn 2013.
21. Quoted in Wilton 1987, p. 62.
22. Scott 1857, Canto III, p. 433, n. 3.
23. Turner's first experience of a coaching accident occurred on 15 January 1820, when his carriage capsized on the Mont Cenis Pass. It is memorialised in a watercolour: *Snow Storm, Mont Cenis* (1820, Birmingham City Museum and Art Gallery).
24. Turner to Charles Lock Eastlake, February 1829, in Gage 1980, pp. 125–6.
25. Turner sketched his coach being 'dug out of a ditch between Ghent and Bruge' in 1824 (Rylance-Watson 2014A).
26. On the role of 'misadventure' narratives in the personae of the Romantic traveller, see Thompson 2007, pp. 1–5, 26–30.
27. Warrell 2012, pp. 10, 140–1.
28. Warrell 2012, pp. 133–4, and Imms 2018.
29. In 1802 he was accompanied in Switzerland by Newbey Lowson (1773–1853), who provided a private coach and guide. H.A.J. Munro of Novar (1797–1864) sponsored his 1833 and 1836 continental trips, joining him on the second (Powell in Joll, Butlin and Herrmann 2001, p. 342).
30. Imms 2011 and Jacklin 2018.
31. Powell 1982.
32. *Route to Rome* sketchbook, Tate, London (CLXXI 35a; D13926).
33. London 1991–2.
34. CXVI 9 and 270; Tate D19568 and D20080.
35. CCCXLIV d 426; Tate D34922. Warrell 1997, p. 22.
36. XLVI 120; Tate D02176.
37. Cook and Wedderburn 1903–12, vol. XIII, p. 474.
38. John Ruskin made the first inventory of Turner's sketches, noting his habit of folding large sheets of paper into four as 'Turner's favourite mode of packing for travelling'. Quoted in Thornbury 1897, p. 386.
39. Warrell 2014.
40. Finberg 1961, p. 262.
41. Cyrus Redding, quoted in Thornbury 1877, pp. 143–4.
42. Rylance-Watson 2014B.
43. London, Mannheim and Hamburg 1995–6, p. 55.
44. Butlin and Joll 1984, p. 126, no. 231.
45. Rylance-Watson 2013.
46. Imms 2017.
47. Turner to John James Ruskin, 15 May 1845, in Gage 1980, p. 206, letter 282.
48. Chu 2013.
49. Boase and Brown 2004.
50. Ritchie 1835, p. 188.
51. Ritchie 1833, p. 12.
52. Ibid. p. 18.
53. Recollected by Rev. William Kingsley and transcribed in Ruskin 1856–7, p. 73.
54. Levitine 1967.

CATALOGUE ENTRIES
Aimee Ng

CAT. 1

1. Turner's trip took place from 10 August to 15 September 1824. On Turner's travels on the continent see especially London 1991–2 and London, Mannheim and Hamburg 1995–6.
2. This conflict (1688–97) saw a coalition of European states allied against France during the reign of Louis XIV.
3. Sadler 1869, vol. 2, p. 20.
4. For interpretations of the subtitle see Galassi in New York 2017, p. 107, n. 34; Nottingham, Hull and Hastings 2008–9, p. 27; London, Minneapolis and New York 2003–4, p. 201.
5. On John Broadhurst see New York 2017, pp. 147–8.
6. The third Turner was *Guardship at the Nore, Sheerness, &c.* (exh. 1809; private collection).
7. See Willis 1854, p. 44, and Dibdin 1829, p. 5.
8. See Galassi in New York 2017, p. 148.

CAT. 2

1. On Turner and Cologne, see Cologne 1980.
2. London, Mannheim and Hamburg 1995–6, pp. 33–4.
3. *Great St Martin's Church and Rhine Gate, Cologne, from the North*, in *Waterloo and Rhine* sketchbook, 1817. Tate, London (D12752; CLX 27a). See Galassi in New York 2017, p. 98; London 1991–2, p. 23. The Stapelhaus ('staple house' or 'stacking house') was originally used for the storage of goods.
4. Galassi in New York 2017, p. 102. On the history of the buildings, see Schäfke 2005, pp. 59–61.
5. Galassi in New York 2017, p. 102.
6. Gage 1980, p. 108, no. 123.
7. Hellen in New York 2017, p. 117.
8. Cook and Wedderburn 1904, vol. 12, pp. 130–1.
9. Byrne 1826.
10. Information regarding Henry Clay Frick's acquisition of the paintings comes from correspondence in the Frick's curatorial files.

SELECTED BIBLIOGRAPHY

ARDILL 2010
T. Ardill, 'Tour of Scotland for Scott's *Poetical Works* 1831', August 2010, rev. M. Imms, September 2016, in Brown 2012–, www.tate.org.uk/art/research-publications/jmw-turner/tour-of-scotland-for-scotts-poetical-works-r1136022 (accessed 14 April 2022)

BALZARETTI, PIANA AND WATKINS 2015
R. Balzaretti, P. Piana and C. Watkins, 'Travelling in Italy during Turner's Lifetime', in Brown 2012–, www.tate.org.uk/art/research-publications/jmw-turner/ross-balzaretti-pietro-piana-and-charles-watkins-travelling-in-italy-during-turners-r1176438 (accessed 14 April 2022)

BOASE AND BROWN 2004
G.C. Boase and D. Brown, 'Ritchie, (Duncan) Leitch (1797–1865), novelist and journalist', *Oxford Dictionary of National Biography*, Oxford 2004

BROWN 2012
D.B. Brown, 'Project Overview', December 2012, in Brown 2012–, www.tate.org.uk/art/research-publications/jmw-turner/project-overview-r1109225 (accessed 14 April 2022)

BROWN 2012–
D.B. Brown (ed.), *J.M.W. Turner: Sketchbooks, Drawings and Watercolours*, Tate Research Publication, December 2012 onwards (accessed 14 April 2022)

BUTLIN AND JOLL 1984
M. Butlin and E. Joll, *The Paintings of J.M.W. Turner*, 2 vols (*Text* and *Plates*), New Haven and London 1984

BYRNE 1826
N. Byrne, 'Royal Academy', *The Morning Post*, 9 May 1826

CHU 2013
J. Chu, 'A Harpooned Whale 1845 by Joseph Mallord William Turner', catalogue entry, December 2013, in Brown 2012–, www.tate.org.uk/art/research-publications/jmw-turner/joseph-mallord-william-turner-a-harpooned-whale-r1173490 (accessed 14 April 2022)

COLOGNE 1980
A. von der Borch, *J.M. William Turner, Köln und der Rhein: Aquarelle, Zeichnungen, Skizzenbücher, Stiche*, exh. cat., Wallraf-Richartz-Museum, Cologne 1980

COOK AND WEDDERBURN 1903–12
E.T. Cook and A. Wedderburn (eds), *The Library Edition of the Works of John Ruskin*, London 1903–12

COOK AND WEDDERBURN 1904
E.T. Cook and A. Wedderburn (eds), *The Works of John Ruskin*, London 1904

DIBDIN 1829
T.F. Dibdin, *A Bibliographical, Antiquarian and Picturesque Tour in France and Germany*, vol. 1, London 1829

EGERTON 1998
J. Egerton, *National Gallery Catalogues: The British Paintings*, London 1998

FINBERG 1961
A.J. Finberg, *The Life of J.M.W. Turner, RA*, Oxford 1961

FINLEY 1980
G. Finley, *Landscapes of Memory: Turner as Illustrator to Scott*, London 1980

GAGE 1980
J. Gage (ed.), *Collected Correspondence of J.M.W. Turner: With an Early Diary and a Memoir by George Jones*, Oxford 1980

GILPIN 1792
W. Gilpin, *Three Essays: On Picturesque Beauty; On Picturesque Travel; and on Sketching Landscape: To Which Is Added a Poem, on Landscape Painting*, London 1792

HILL 1992
D. Hill, *Turner in the Alps: The Journey through France and Switzerland in 1802*, Goring-by-Sea 1992

IMMS 2011
M. Imms, '*Devonshire Coast, No.1* sketchbook 1811', June 2011, in Brown 2012–, www.tate.org.uk/art/research-publications/jmw-turner/devonshire-coast-no1-sketchbook-r1136835 (accessed 14 April 2022)

IMMS 2017
M. Imms, '*Venice: San Giorgio Maggiore – Early Morning* 1819 by Joseph Mallord William Turner', catalogue entry, March 2017, in Brown 2012–, www.tate.org.uk/art/research-publications/jmw-turner/joseph-mallord-william-turner-venice-san-giorgio-maggiore-early-morning-r1186394 (accessed 14 April 2022)

IMMS 2018
M. Imms, '*Two Semi-Clad Women at a Window in Venice, Conversing with Men Below* 1840 by Joseph Mallord William Turner', catalogue entry, September 2018, in Brown 2012–, www.tate.org.uk/art/research-publications/jmw-turner/joseph-mallord-william-turner-two-semi-clad-women-at-a-window-in-venice-conversing-with-r1196474 (accessed 14 April 2022)

JACKLIN 2018
E. Jacklin, 'Reichard's "Italy", with Sketches and Inscriptions by Turner c.1819 by Joseph Mallord William Turner', catalogue entry, September 2018, in Brown 2012–, www.tate.org.uk/art/research-publications/jmw-turner/joseph-mallord-william-turner-reichards-italy-with-sketches-and-inscriptions-by-turner-r1195560 (accessed 14 April 2022)

JOLL, BUTLIN AND HERRMANN 2001
E. Joll, M. Butlin and L. Herrmann (eds), *The Oxford Companion to J.M.W. Turner*, Oxford 2001

LASSELS 1670
R. Lassels, *The Voyage of Italy: Or, A Compleat Journey through Italy. In Two Parts. With the Characters of the People, and the Description of the Chief Towns, Churches, Monasteries, Tombs, Libraries, Pallaces, Villas, Gardens, Pictures, Statues, and Antiquities. As also of the Interest, Government, Riches, Force, &c. of all the Princes; With Instructions Concerning Travel*, Paris 1670

LEVITINE 1967
G. Levitine, 'Vernet Tied to a Mast in a Storm: The Evolution of an Episode of Art Historical Romantic Folklore', *The Art Bulletin*, 49, no. 2 (1967), pp. 93–100

LONDON 1991–2
C. Powell, *Turner's Rivers of Europe: The Rhine, Meuse and Mosel*, exh. cat., Tate Gallery, London 1991–2

LONDON 2000
R. Hewison, *Ruskin, Turner and the Pre-Raphaelites*, exh. cat., Tate Britain, London 2000

LONDON 2012
I. Warrell et al., *Turner Inspired: In the Light of Claude*, exh. cat., The National Gallery, London 2012

LONDON 2013
C. Riding and R. Johns, *Turner and the Sea*, exh. cat., National Maritime Museum, London 2013

LONDON, MANNHEIM AND HAMBURG 1995–6
C. Powell, *Turner in Germany*, exh. cat., Tate Gallery, London; Städtische Kunsthalle, Mannheim; Hamburger Kunsthalle 1995–6

LONDON, MINNEAPOLIS AND NEW YORK 2003–4
P. Noon (ed.), *Constable to Delacroix: British Art and the French Romantics*, exh. cat., Tate Britain, London; Minneapolis Institute of Arts; Metropolitan Museum of Art, New York 2003–4

LONDON, PHILADELPHIA AND MINNEAPOLIS 2002
A. Wilton and T. Barringer, *American Sublime: Landscape Painting in the United States 1820–1880*, exh. cat., Tate Britain, London; Pennsylvania Academy of the Fine Arts, Philadelphia; Minneapolis Institute of Arts 2002

NEW YORK 2017
S.G. Galassi, I. Warrell and J. Sheers Seidenstein, *Turner's Modern and Ancient Ports: Passages through Time*, exh. cat., The Frick Collection, New York 2017

NEW YORK 2018
E.M. Kornhauser, T.J. Barringer, D. Mahon et al., *Thomas Cole's Journey: Atlantic Crossings*, Metropolitan Museum of Art, New York 2018

NOTTINGHAM, HULL AND HASTINGS 2008–9
D.B. Brown, S. Skinner and I. Warrell, *Coasting: Turner and Bonington on the Shores of the Channel*, exh. cat., Nottingham Castle; Ferens Art Gallery, Hull; Hastings Museum and Art Gallery 2008–9

POWELL 1982
C. Powell, 'Topography, Imagination and Travel: Turner's Relationship with James Hakewill', *Art History*, 5, no. 4 (1982)

RIDING AND LLEWELLYN 2013
C. Riding and N. Llewellyn, 'British Art and the Sublime', in N. Llewellyn and C. Riding (eds), *The Art of the Sublime*, Tate Research Publication, January 2013, www.tate.org.uk/art/research-publications/the-sublime/christine-riding-and-nigel-llewellyn-british-art-and-the-sublime-r1109418 (accessed 14 April 2022)

RITCHIE 1833
L. Ritchie, *Wanderings by the Loire, with Twenty-One Engravings from Drawings by J.M.W. Turner*, London 1833

RITCHIE 1835
L. Ritchie, *Wanderings by the Seine, from Rouen to the Source, with Twenty Engravings from Drawings by J.M.W. Turner*, London 1835

RUSKIN 1856–7
J. Ruskin, *Notes on the Turner Collection at Marlborough House*, 5th ed., London 1856–7

RYLANCE-WATSON 2013
A. Rylance-Watson, 'Trèves and Rhine Sketchbook 1824', December 2013, in Brown 2012–, www.tate.org.uk/art/research-publications/jmw-turner/treves-and-rhine-sketchbook-r1174876 (accessed 14 April 2022)

RYLANCE-WATSON 2014A
A. Rylance-Watson, '*An Accident to a Diligence between Ghent and Bruges* 1824 by Joseph Mallord William Turner', catalogue entry, June 2014, in Brown 2012–, www.tate.org.uk/art/research-publications/jmw-turner/joseph-mallord-william-turner-an-accident-to-a-diligence-between-ghent-and-bruges-r1174656 (accessed 14 April 2022)

RYLANCE-WATSON 2014B
A. Rylance-Watson, 'The First Meuse-Moselle Tour 1824', June 2014, in Brown 2012–, www.tate.org.uk/art/research-publications/jmw-turner/the-first-meuse-moselle-tour-r1175013 (accessed 14 April 2022)

SADLER 1869
T. Sadler (ed.), *Diary, Reminiscences, and Correspondence of Henry Crabb Robinson*, 2 vols, Boston 1869

SCHÄFKE 2005
W. Schäfke, *Köln von seiner schönsten Seite*, Cologne 2005

SCOTT 1857
Sir W. Scott, *The Poetical Works of Sir Walter Scott*, vol. 10, Edinburgh 1857

SHANES 1981
E. Shanes, *Turner's Rivers, Harbours and Coasts*, London 1981

SHANES 2016
E. Shanes, *Young Mr Turner: The First Forty Years, 1775–1815*, New Haven and London 2016

SWEET 2012
R. Sweet, *Cities and the Grand Tour: The British in Italy, c.1690–1820*, Cambridge 2012

THOMPSON 2007
C. Thompson, *The Suffering Traveller and the Romantic Imagination*, Oxford 2007

THORNBURY 1877
W. Thornbury, *The Life of J.M.W. Turner, RA*, London 1877

THORNBURY 1897
W. Thornbury, *The Life of J.M.W. Turner, RA*, rev. ed., London 1897

UNWINS 1858
S. Unwins, *A Memoir of Thomas Unwins, RA*, vol. 2, London 1858

WARRELL 1997
I. Warrell, *Turner on the Loire*, London 1997

WARRELL 1999
I. Warrell, *Turner on the Seine*, London 1999

WARRELL 2012
I. Warrell, *Turner's Secret Sketches*, London 2012

WARRELL 2014
I. Warrell, *Turner's Sketchbooks*, London 2014

WASHINGTON, DC, DALLAS AND NEW YORK 2007
I. Warrell (ed.), *J.M.W. Turner*, exh. cat., National Gallery of Art, Washington, DC; Dallas Museum of Art; Metropolitan Museum of Art, New York, 2007

WILLIS 1854
G. Willis, *Willis's Current Notes*, May 1854

WILTON 1979
A. Wilton, *J.M.W. Turner: His Art and Life*, Fribourg 1979

WILTON 1981
A. Wilton, *Turner and the Sublime*, Chicago 1981

WILTON 1987
A. Wilton, *Turner in His Time*, New York 1987

WILTON 2013
A. Wilton, 'Preliminary Study for *Calais Pier, with French Poissards Preparing for Sea: An English Packet Arriving* c.1802 by Joseph Mallord William Turner', catalogue entry, May 2013, in Brown 2012–, www.tate.org.uk/art/research-publications/jmw-turner/joseph-mallord-william-turner-preliminary-study-for-calais-pier-with-french-poissards-r1178164 (accessed 14 April 2022)

WINE 2001
H. Wine, *National Gallery Catalogues: The Seventeenth-Century French Paintings*, London 2001

Tate holds a collection of Turner's sketchbooks as part of the Turner Bequest in 1856. Many can be accessed online: www.tate.org.uk/search?q=turner+sketchbook

PHOTOGRAPHIC CREDITS

EDINBURGH
Scottish National Gallery © National Galleries of Scotland: fig. 20.

HAMBURG
Hamburger Kunsthalle, Hamburg © Bridgeman Images: fig. 21.

LONDON
The British Museum, London © The Trustees of the British Museum: fig. 22.
© The National Gallery, London: figs 2, 10, 16, 17, 19.
© Royal Academy of Arts, London: fig. 13.
© Tate: cats 1.2, 2.2; figs 9, 14, 15, 23, 24, 25, 26.
Victoria and Albert Museum, London © V&A Images / Victoria and Albert Museum, London: fig. 18.

MAINZ
Rheinisches Landesmuseum, Bonn © akg images: fig. 6.

MANCHESTER
Manchester Art Gallery © Manchester City Galleries / Bridgeman Images: fig. 8.

NEW HAVEN, CONNECTICUT
© Yale Center for British Art: figs 1, 7, 12.

NEW YORK
The Frick Collection, New York © The Frick Collection, New York / photo: Michael Bodycomb: front and back cover; cats 1, 2; pp. 2, 3, 6, 44–5, 64; detail photography of cats 1, 2 © The Frick Collection, New York / photo: Joseph Coscia Jr.
The New-York Historical Society, New York © Collection of The New-York Historical Society, New York. Digital image created by Oppenheimer Editions: fig. 11.

PRIVATE COLLECTIONS
Private collection © Agnew's, London / Bridgeman Images: fig. 4.

SEATTLE, WASHINGTON
The Seattle Art Museum © The Seattle Art Museum / Bridgeman Images: fig. 3.

WASHINGTON, DC
National Gallery of Art, Washington, DC. Photo Courtesy National Gallery of Art, Washington: fig. 5.

ACKNOWLEDGEMENTS

In addition to the comments made in the Directors' Foreword, I would like to add my own heartfelt thanks to Ian Wardropper, Xavier F. Salomon and Aimee Ng at The Frick Collection. At the National Gallery, I am especially grateful to Robyn Earl for her management of the exhibition, and to Justine Rinnooy Kan for her support and advice, as well as Chris Oberon and Louise Nyborg for their striking exhibition design, and to Lydia Cooper for her sensitive handling of the exhibition interpretation. The accompanying catalogue has been a truly collaborative effort, designed by Adrian Hunt and copy-edited by Camilla Rockwood, and overseen with care and attention by Catherine Hooper, Jane Hyne, Suzanne Bosman and other colleagues at National Gallery Global. I am also grateful to Thomas Ardill and Aimee Ng for their insightful contributions to the catalogue, and for their encouragement throughout. Finally, I would like to acknowledge the following individuals for their assistance in matters relating to the exhibition and catalogue: Caroline Campbell, Emma Capron, Neil Evans, Anne Fay, Julie Firth, Tracy Jones, Joseph Kendra, Laura Lappin, Simon Magill, Alexandra Moskalenko, Patrick O'Sullivan, John Shevlin and Belinda Phillpot.

CHRISTINE RIDING

(OVERLEAF) Detail of cat. 2

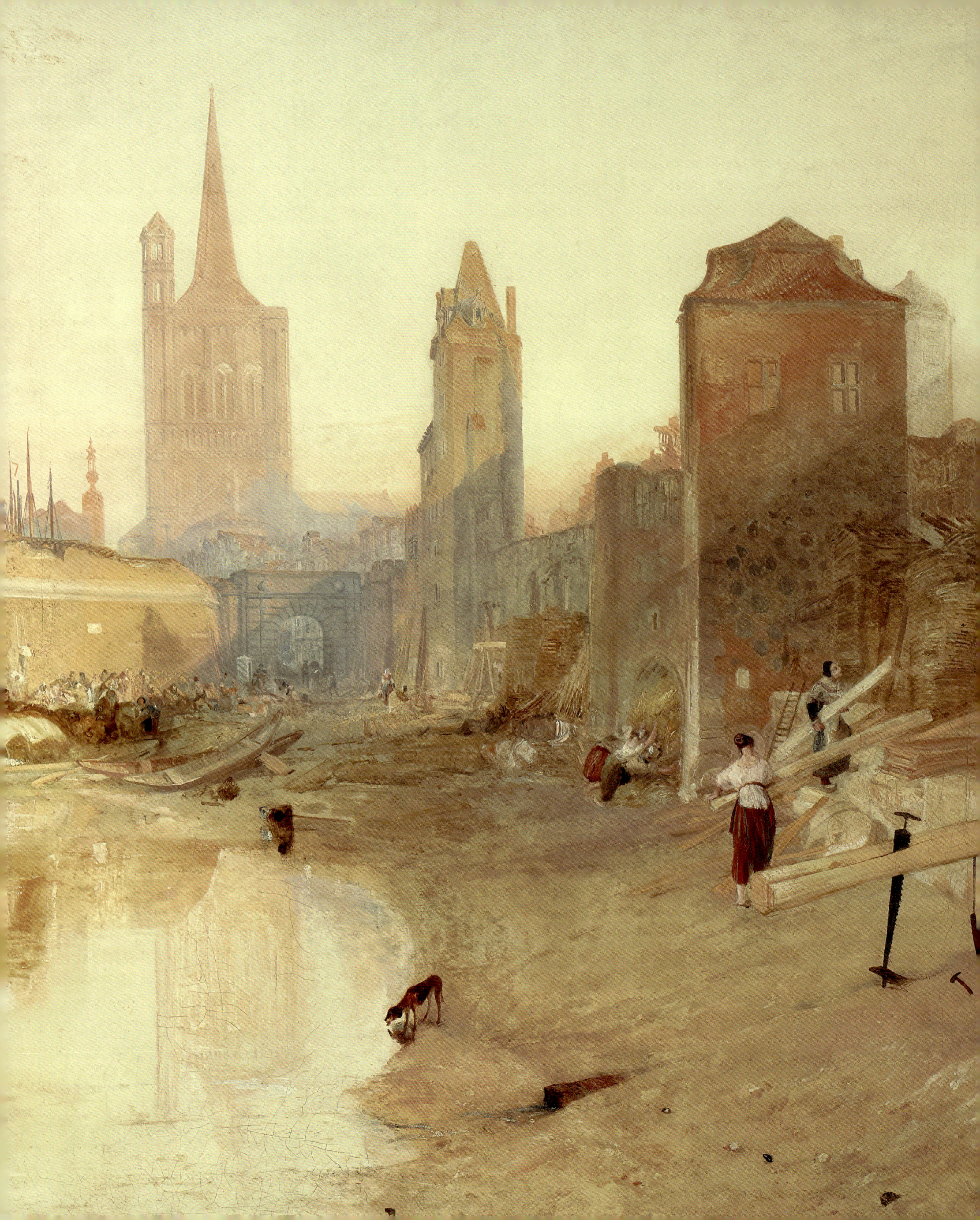